Daylight Robbery!

Alan Crossland

First published 2002 by Acorn Publications, Newark

ISBN: 1 903263 59 X

Daylight Robbery!

Index

Chapter	*Title*	*Page*
	Prologue	5
1.	What's it all about?	7
2.	Fact or fiction	12
3.	Thin end of the Wedge	17
4.	Bricks & Mortar	22
5.	Whose fault is it anyway?	30
6.	The trouble with people is.	41
7.	Wild Goose chase?	51
8.	Handpicked	58
9.	Goal !	64
	Epilogue	75

Daylight Robbery!

Prologue

Since the advent of Christendom untold numbers of books have been written with the sole idea of establishing men, women and children in The Faith. Scholars far cleverer and much more learned than I have sought by one means or another to encourage the believer along the Christian pathway.

Yet despite this indisputable fact, it is true to say that so many do miss the mark and are virtually robbed of the treasures God the Father has for His children.

My writings in this book will add to the millions of words already written in an attempt to help, maybe in a minute way at least one person enter into this spiritual Aladdin's cave and receive from the hand of God what He has promised to those who in all sincerity seek to follow Christ. It is an attempt to clear away just a few of the myths and misunderstandings which present a barrier to the fulfilment of these promises.

I have limited my writings to the use of one book only, namely the Bible for my authority in the statements made. Whilst I have personally benefited enormously by the contributions other Christian writers may have made - and they certainly have opened doors to thoughts and ideas I think I would have missed - the words in this book are as a result of Bible study and having, I believe the aid of the Holy Spirit to interpret. Allying this with common sense, personal experience, logic, instinct and interpreting *all* Scripture in the spirit of Christ the end result has been the writing of *'Daylight Robbery!'* To be robbed of all He has for us is surely the biggest crime ever committed and sometimes, regrettably, we are the ones at fault.

To be a follower of Jesus Christ is not the miserable chore which some people would have us believe. On the contrary it is the most fulfilling and joyous experience man can ever hope for. Jesus Himself stated that He came to bring us life, ABUNDANT life. (John 10: 10)

There is no attempt to open up a deep theological discussion or doctrinal discourse (I could not do this even if I tried!), and I trust the words written will find no argument with the beliefs held by other Christians. It is just a desire to put into layman's terms an acceptable and sensible answer to a number of issues which can cause problems to an aspiring follower of Christ.

Of course there will always be unanswered questions in such a quest. There will always be mysteries which cannot be answered in this life and which have puzzled and exercised the mind of mankind since he became aware of the existence of God. This has to be. If we knew all there was about God and His ways He wouldn't be God, but as suggested by Dr. Leslie Wetherhead, the highly respected and deeply spiritual Methodist minister, what we cannot understand at the time, we must simply place into a drawer of our mind, to be opened at a later stage in our experience.

If the words penned assist one of my brothers or sisters in Christ into a more fulfilling experience I will feel the effort of writing has been worthwhile, and give God the glory.

Alan Crossland
March 2002

1. What's it all about?

To make any sense of becoming a Christian and living a Christian life, one really has to understand the underlying reason for our existence. Why should we bother, what is the purpose of it all?

'Let's start at the very beginning, a very good place to start' so sings Maria in the musical, *'The Sound of Music'.* It is to our advantage to take her advice when dealing with the most fundamental, important issue mankind can ever seek to consider.

However we might interpret the momentous happenings described in the Bible and known to us as *'The Fall,'* Gen.3, there is little doubt that early man quickly moved from his privileged place of close communion with God to being shut out from His presence. This was the wilful act of going against all the good advice God had given him to ensure a happy and fulfilling life. The entry of SIN into this hitherto beautiful sinless world made the difference. Sin brought with it so many unpleasant things, and was the automatic reward, compared (as Paul writes) with that of receiving wages for employment, and includes things such as lying, deceit, selfishness, sickness and so on until death, Romans 6: 23 *(first part of verse)* which, up to this point had not existed.

But it also brought something else, *separation* from God. This state of existence, brought about by disobedience, hurt God as much as it did man yet right at the very beginning He put into operation a plan to redress the situation, which would not compromise with sin, but rather deal with it honourably and completely. Gen. 3: 15 & John 3: 16 .

Thus the plan of *reconciliation* came into being, with God actively taking the initiative to bring mankind back to the relationship he had previously enjoyed. 2 Cor. 5: 19 and it wasn't a restoration brought about by any effort on our part but was a gift from God *(second half of Romans 6: 23, see also John 3: 16)* When the jailor asked Paul and Silas what did he have to do to be saved, Paul said in effect nothing, but believe. (Acts 16: 31) In other words, God had done all there was to actually *do,* all man had to do now was to make a conscious effort to *believe,* and this would ensure he received God's plan of salvation.

It really is as simple as that, perhaps too simple for some people but acceptance through our belief, opens a door to a life which is almost too wonderful and breath-taking for the mind to comprehend. Beautiful though it may be, the English language is most inadequate in trying to describe what actually takes place when we are made 'at one' with God, there simply aren't sufficient words at our disposal to do this justice. *'It's better felt than telt,'* is an old Yorkshire saying, suggesting the experience of salvation goes deeper than mere words.

Believing in Jesus is a startling, illuminating, and humbling experience. Becoming aware of Jesus one can see the contrast in His goodness and our sinfulness, and we are ashamed at such a revelation. Even those who may never have committed any great wilful wrongdoing (sin) still become aware they are far removed from what they ought to be, and their lives have been lived which has caused hurt to others, to themselves and now they are aware has caused hurt to God.

This belief quickens the conscience, and we *feel* guilty for our wrong doing. We *feel* we are accountable to God and yet need to deal with this guilt. Perhaps in the past when there have been those pangs of conscience, we have tried to make amends by turning over a new leaf or making a new year's resolution but how long do these last? And do they deal with our guilt? Of course not.

But when we accept Christ into our lives, when we confess our wrongdoing and ask Him to forgive us, in a miraculous way our guilt *is* dealt with. (1 John 1 : 9) We recognise His death on the cross dealt with completely our sin and its consequences. We discovered He *does* forgive and untold numbers of Christians will testify to a feeling to be described only *as "A great burden being lifted from one's back"* and *"as though a person was walking on air."*

The unbelievable has taken place, we become aware that God is a *living* Being, we feel He is interested in us and that the break, made by our first parents has now been healed.

Reconciliation has been made between the believer and the Father.(2 Cor. 5: 19) The love for His children was and is so immense that He took upon Himself all the sin and guilt of the world. It was nailed to the cross on that first Good Friday, the cross became the bridge, linking once again the created with their Creator.

The motivation behind living now becomes God-centred and not self-centred. Pleasing Him becomes our greatest desire and bringing him hurt becomes abhorrent to our thinking.

It does have to be the real thing though. Many a person may have, to all intents and appearances become a Christian, yet their lives do not confirm this and we are told that, *'By their fruits shall we know them."* (Matt. 7: 15-20) In other words, their lives do not indicate they are any different to the non-believer.

A national leader of one of our evangelical churches caused a considerable amount of consternation when he declared, in conference with hundreds of its full time ministers that there were some of those present in the lecture hall who were not converted! What a statement to be made to a group of evangelists! One can imagine how this statement was received, yet listening afterwards to the comments made by some who had been present only confirmed that what he said did have an element of truth in the words uttered.

In a perfect situation, all members of the Church, including its leaders, (and this includes the Army) are soundly converted, born again, changed – call it what we like. In practice though we know it is so easily possible to *appear* to fulfil all the necessary obligations to being a Christian and yet missing out on this basic experience. (Titus 1: 16)

In my own experience, and in my forty-two years in Army ministry, I have observed, sadly, all too often where this is true. Good people, gifted and capable, having been sent to Sunday school very early in their lives. Taking an active part in the programme offered by the church or corps. Ready to support financially in every way and yet regrettably missing out upon God's promises because tragically, they have never been really reconciled with God. Looking the part may be a good thing, but it is *being* rather than looking that is important.

I recall my very first appointment after being commissioned (ordained) as an officer. It was a small group of people I was called upon to minister to in South London, but they were all working class people and at that time in the late 1950s, money was rather scarce. They could not afford to have fresh flowers each week to adorn the Holiness Table and so someone had the bright idea of having in the cupboard a vase of plastic flowers, which could be used when the real thing was missing. It made a splash of colour but there was no comparison to the real thing.

There can be no 'artificial' experience of God. It just has to be the real thing and if we settle for anything less we are being robbed and need to do something about it, no matter what our age.

Before one goes any further, one must ask God, through Christ to *really* come to us, to forgive our wrongdoing, to restore us to that rightful place of being a child of God and to take control of our lives. Having made this prayer, one needs to *believe* He has done this for us. Then, accept the transformation has taken place, no matter whether we *feel* any different from before. If we do our part, and this includes prayer, searching the Scriptures and making a firm effort to accept responsibility for our actions, He certainly will do His. He will confirm or give *assurance* that we have been reconciled to Him, accepted into His family even though there may be a delay before receiving this from His hand.

It cannot be emphasised too much, that conversion really does mean a healing of the terrible break made when sin entered the world. No longer strangers or aliens, but children of the living God. *Reconciled* with our Heavenly Father. Brought back into the family, restored to our rightful, God-intended place.

From now on, there is a growing loving relationship. There will be 'ups and downs' but maintaining and developing this relationship becomes an adventure – at times a mind boggling adventure of, (to coin another musical) *'Getting to know You.'*

Making such a statement does appear to be unattainable at first and I know many, many people just will not understand and so

reject this possibility. I can only speak from personal experience and so this statement can be accepted or rejected as you will. It does not alter the fact as far as I am concerned.
It is a further remarkable fact that such an indescribable experience transcends all denominational persuasions too. I venture to say, when a man, woman or child is reconciled with the Lord one sees each other as brothers and sisters in Christ and the 'labels' we might put on each other are of little importance, and certainly no barrier to sweet fellowship.

But all is not well, because by deliberately taking this step we have invited the full onslaught of an untiring enemy who will do all he can to drive a wedge, create a gulf or chasm between my newly found Friend (Jesus) and me. The Devil is quite open and brazen about this. The act of reconciliation may have set the bells ringing in Heaven and the angels rejoicing (Luke 15: 7,10.) but the Devil is not amused and will seek every way possible to turn us away from God. If we do not stay alert and watch and pray he will commit robbery, daylight robbery and take away all God has prepared for us.

2. Fact or Fiction

From observation, it is painfully true that far too many people who would call themselves Christians have never had any *real* assurance that a change has taken place and that they have been made *right* before God. What a tragedy! How can such good folk be expected to live a Christian life when denied this all important blessing?

Let us examine carefully the meaning of *assurance* when referring to the life of the Spirit. After all, if we are not sure what we are speaking about how can we be expected to enter into this blessed experience?

My dictionary states that the word, *assure* means *'to make safe; secure; certain; to give confidence to; to encourage'* and *assurance* means *'a positive declaration; certainty, security; reliance; intrepidity.'*

It was during the centenary celebrations of The Salvation Army and held in the Royal Albert Hall in the presence of H.M. The Queen, the then Archbishop of Canterbury made a statement which caught the imagination and approval of all present. Dr. Michael Ramsey declared in his words of greeting, *"I have travelled the world, and seen many strange and wonderful things, but one thing I have never seen is a miserable Salvationist!"* You can imagine there was a tremendous response to such complimentary words. However, later that day, when such specially invited guests were no longer present, the General made reference to these very words. *"How wonderful to learn that the Archbishop has never seen a miserable Salvationist,"* he said, then with a twinkle in his eye went on to say, *"he obviously hasn't visited some of the places I have!"*

The point being made surely is that our expression of Christianity is marked by *joy,* and real joy can only come when there is assurance, deep within one's heart and soul that all is well with God and that no matter what may happen today or in the future, I am safe and secure in His hands. (Romans 8: 38-39)

To be a real Christian one has discovered the secret of deep-down joy, joy which *no* experience in life, no matter how devastating, can take away or interfere with.

I personally recall a long list of men and women I have known who have proved this to be true and who have been a source of challenge and encouragement to me. Heading this list is a lady I used to visit at frequent intervals in the hospital. A woman in her mid fifties but hospitalised for over ten years due to unbelievable arthritis. Her limbs were so distorted and deformed. A constant battle with bed sores. Having hardly any flesh upon her crooked frame of a body making every movement, however slight, a painful operation, yet did she complain? Not on your life. She was bubbling over with the joy of her Lord. It wasn't that she was insensitive to pain, not at all, but her closeness with her Lord and Saviour transcended the pain, took her beyond it. She knew she could rest, content in Him and knowing that one day she would share His glory and be free of all the limitations of this life. Needless to say, although the idea of a visit was to bring blessing to her, I was the one who gained the most blessing.

She had what all true believers have had since Christ came into the world.

She shared what the first Christian martyr Stephen, experienced as he faced certain death, (Acts 7) when he asked God to forgive his killers even as he knelt and took his last breath (v 60) It was the same kind of experience Paul and Silas shared when wrongly suffering in a dungeon after being flogged and chained (Acts 16: 25) They didn't wallow in self pity but sang praises to God. They were so full of joy. They had *assurance* that all was well deep within their souls and this has been the hall-mark of Christians throughout the centuries, much to the annoyance of their enemies. Even when faced by ferocious lions they have stood firm, they *knew* without a doubt they were secure in the hands of their Lord. And it wasn't a second-hand assurance, it was really personal. Head knowledge, gained by reading or being told by another, moved a further step forward to become *heart* knowledge. There is a difference. Neither was this some kind of indoctrination or disillusionment. Prompted by love for their Lord they received, deep down the conviction, the 'feeling', the 'gut-reaction' they were completely safe in the hands of Jesus. In other words, they had this *blessed assurance* which we sing about, and which turns an otherwise weak, timid person into one which, if necessary will face suffering, even death for their Lord.

It is plain to see that such an experience, whilst touching the emotions transcends them. When I was a Boy Scout I had to learn the ten laws all members of the movement learned. One law included the words, *'A Scout smiles and whistles under all difficulties.'* We know what this suggests to the Boy Scout. A Christian has a similar attitude. This does not mean they take possession of a kind of porcelain grin and walk about with the head in the clouds, or to coin a phrase, "Being so heavenly minded they are of no earthly use!" of course not. One still feels pain, still suffers disappointments, misunderstandings etc., in common with all mankind, but it does mean one sees these for what they are, temporal, passing experiences and discovers God turns these stumbling blocks to our equilibrium, into stepping stones to serenity of spirit and character building. Many people link up with the church and find the friendly fellowship and the active programme does fulfil a gap in their lives as it often gives an avenue for them to use any gifts they might possess. Maybe comparable to a social club. I have no real argument to this but if we leave it at that and do not go any further we do a grave injustice to the Gospel and rob ourselves of the best and settle for a second best experience. It means too that when life's tests come along (as they surely will) this second best will not carry us through.

No wonder then so many Christians do become disillusioned, bitter and often give up their fight as a Christian. I would be the same. Without this assurance, how can one believe in an all-loving, all-powerful victorious God? Without this assurance we are confronted with all sorts of problems and difficulties and life does not make sense. True, we may not have *all* the answers but this will not worry us unduly. Without this assurance our involvement in the life of our church will in the end become a chore and lose its attraction.

There is a little children's song known to most church-goers. *'I am so glad that Jesus loves me.'* One verse states, *'If one should ask of me, how could I tell? Glory to Jesus, I know very well. God's Holy Spirit with mine doth agree, constantly witnessing, Jesus loves me.'*

These words are echoing those written by Paul and found in the book of Romans, *'The Spirit testifies with our spirit, that we are the children of God.'* (Rom. 8: 16) They indicate that such a confirmation is readily provided by God and automatically available once we believe. We have our faith rewarded by actually *knowing* or being *convinced* it is true. Alleluia!

It is an ever present temptation to judge our religious experience upon how we *'feel'*. This is quite dangerous and can trip us up badly for our feelings are so fickle, being affected by so many outside influences. But having said this, there will be times when we actually feel in our bones, the very presence of God and how blest and encouraged we are when this happens.

We come back to what has already been stated. To receive this assurance our repentance and faith must be genuine. Without genuine repentance there can be no genuine forgiveness. Without forgiveness, there can be no assurance.

If your religion is going to be real and vibrant, you cannot be satisfied with anything less. Remember this really is for *you.* Not just for those who may be gifted or clever but for *all* who believe. (John 3: 15-16)

This is no passport into escapism. You will have your share of life's trials, yet, despite the tears which may come you will not be moved. Deep down you will remain secure and unshakable.

Like so many of my colleague officers, I have conducted untold numbers of funerals and have always endeavoured to bring comfort to the bereaved. I have observed however, with genuine sadness, those who have no faith experience despair, yet those who know God, despite the loss see victory beyond the grave. They possess a buoyancy denied to the non-believer.

Having therefore established a relationship with the living Lord the Christian will now seek, not just to maintain this relationship but to develop it, and so there begins an adventure which lasts a life-time and beyond. A relationship which on occasions is buffeted by the storms of life but remains secure.

3. Thin end of the Wedge

With our newly found Companion, we commence life's adventure and what a tale so many of us could tell! But sharing this with Jesus, the richness of life is enhanced beyond all recognition and we anticipate that glorious occasion keenly when we will see Him face to face.

Reference has already been made to problems and pitfalls we will encounter on the way. Jesus never ever hinted that to be a follower of His will ensure a calm, peaceful, untroubled 'bed of roses' and those of us who have been travelling any length of time will confirm these words. On the contrary, our introduction to the living Lord also makes us aware of the existence of the Evil One who is far from being thrilled at our newly found faith.

To be forewarned is to be forearmed so they say. I need to warn any and every budding Christian that for the rest of your life you will suffer at the hands of the Devil. His prime purpose will be to drive a wedge between you and God. Make no mistake about this! Trusting in God brings the believer at last into eternal happiness. If the Devil can turn you from this he will and take you with him to Hell!

It would be impossible to list every diabolical way he sets about to do this but apart from having a direct hand in it he does have agents working for him, some unwittingly too. Even our best friends and relatives can be the instruments he will use to achieve his purpose, as Jesus found for Himself with Peter, (Matt. 16: 23) People who ought to know better, our church, our work, our health – you name it – the devil will use it and show no mercy either. He then has the audacity to suggest to our minds that such dastardly acts are instigated by God! Sadly, some believe him. It is therefore to our advantage, in the cool light of day to form a strategy whereby we can deal with these attacks head on and sensibly. It is also to our advantage to consider such possibilities *before* they happen in order to be as prepared as it is possible to be. Waiting until they actually occur and with no preparation puts us at a great disadvantage and we can so easily respond in a most un-Christian way and even have our faith shaken.

Let me remind you again that God's plan for all mankind is for him to be at one with God and that life is a journey of getting to know Him more and more as each day comes. It is an ever growing relationship with the Supreme Being, our Father in Heaven, and the more one knows of Him the more we love Him.

In the final words almost of Jesus to His disciples in the upper room when Thomas was challenged by Jesus, He said, "You believe Me because you have seen Me, but blessed are those who haven't seen Me and believe anyway." (John 20: 29) We further read in a letter by Peter, 'You love Him even though you have never seen Him; though not seeing Him, you trust Him; and even now you are happy with inexpressible joy that comes from heaven itself. And your further reward for trusting Him will be the salvation of your souls.' (1 Peter 1: 8-9)

This love and trust then are the targets of attack but God has not left us defenceless. First of all He has promised to be our constant companion and second, we can be strong enough to resist the temptations put before us and so gain victory.

As with any relationship, we must nurture this carefully and resist any careless or lazy attitude when dealing with God. We need first of all to develop a real prayer life. Any friendship would last for a very limited time if there was never any contact with the parties concerned, yet some people seem to think they can be Christians and rarely if ever do they really speak with God. No wonder He remains almost a stranger to them. This is not what God intends for us. He wants us to know Him as He really is. Just before His death, Jesus gathered His close friends around Him and spent some time speaking about a number of very important issues. (John 13; 14; 15; 16 &17) Now remember, these men had been the closest of companions of the Lord for three years. They had worked, played, talked, walked, prayed, ate, slept, worshipped with Him. They had observed His ministry of healing, His constant friction with those in authority, the miracles all around Palestine. What they didn't know about Jesus was no one's business yet during these final moments. Philip makes a statement which must have cut deep into the heart of Jesus. Jesus' response was, "Don't you even yet know who I am, Philip, even after all this time I have been with you?" (John 14: 9)

It is this personal knowledge which is the all important criteria. Christianity is not a club with a set of rules. It is a living relationship and if our religion is to be meaningful we must seek every way possible to develop and enrich such a relationship. If we neglect prayer, this really is the thin end of the wedge and it won't be long before the gap widens and the latter state will be as bad, if not worse than the former.

One of James Montgomery's hymns include the following words,

'Prayer is the Christian's vital breath,
The Christian's native air,
His watchword at the gates of death;
He enters Heaven with prayer.'

Believers over the years, when suffering persecution particularly have found their very existence and sanity was dependant upon their prayer. Denied access to fellowship and worship with other Christians, the singing of hymns or religious songs, even robbed of the Bible, but relying completely upon the only other means of grace to keep alive one's religious experience – prayer. Many have testified as to how prayer under such circumstances has really come into its own and has become as vital and as precious as the very air we breathe.

Prayer then must head the list. But what is prayer? There are so many mistaken ideas which suggest prayer is either a childish whim or a passing phase, which, when we have grown up and matured grow out of and live without, thank you very much.

My very earliest recollection is that of my mother teaching me at the age of, say two or three years the children's prayer, *'Gentle Jesus, meek and mild; look upon a little child, etc...'*

The trouble is, so many people never progress beyond repeating in parrot like fashion the children's prayer they were taught when they were infants. No wonder it lost its attraction and its place in their lives.

Keeping in mind that our life is one of developing a relationship with God, we must see how prayer will be part of this.

We need to get out of the idea, and pretty quickly too that prayer is a time when we express all our wants, making prayer-time an exercise in 'gimme-gimme-gimme.' It just cannot exist in any real form if that is all it is.

On one occasion, the disciples came to Jesus and asked Him to teach them how to pray as John taught his followers. (Luke 11: 1) and there followed words from Jesus we now call 'The Lord's Prayer'. But to me, such a request by his disciples was a puzzling one because the Jews, of all people, were a nation of pray-ers. Their daily routine included obligatory times of prayer and they were introduced to such a routine at a very early age. If this was so, and it was, why did they ask Jesus to teach them to pray? Surely it was because they observed that Jesus had the secret of prayer. It wasn't for him just a set form of words handed down by the fathers of the nation, even though, as a good Jew he would have used these. No, prayer for Him was close contact with God and one cannot read the Gospels without noticing so plainly that Jesus spent much time in keeping this alive and vital.

He would spend many hours in prayer – communion – contact – with His Father. (Matt. 14: 23; Mark 6: 46; Luke 6: 12 & 9: 28) There were times too when He had 'a quickie' including the time He went to the grave of Lazarus (John 11: 41) In fact, as we become familiar with the life of Jesus we also become aware that He lived in a constant atmosphere of prayer. The important criteria for Him was maintaining the constant and close link with God. No wonder the disciples saw such a marked difference in the prayers *they* had been taught and practiced to that which Jesus embodied. They sensed His prayer life was alive and vital – and they wanted to be like Him.

There is nothing wrong in reciting prayers someone else has written, indeed, to use such prayers can so often introduce one to ideas and thoughts about God which we would have hitherto missed. But we must not limit our prayer life to such 'prepared' prayers. Remember, and this will be repeated a number of times, we are developing a *personal* relationship with God and so, beautiful and helpful though they may be, someone else's prayer will not fill every gap in our search after Him. Our prayers have to come from *our own hearts.*

So how do we set about this? When? Where? What do I say?

4. Bricks & Mortar

Building a relationship with the Living God, like building a house, is serious business and cannot be taken lightly if this is to be worthwhile and fulfilling. We all surely have suffered the loss of friendships due to carelessness or lack of commitment on the part of one party or the other. We cannot really afford to do this with the greatest Friend anyone could have. We must make up our mind that as far as *we* are concerned, we are going to do all we can to make this the most positive and purposeful relationship possible. This means a plan of action and not some 'hitty-missy' approach which is doomed to failure.

As already intimated, prayer heads the list in our relationship building. To begin with, this may appear to be a one-way exercise with you and me being the active participants and no response from the Almighty, but instinct tells us we should pray and when faced with any danger or threatening behaviour from someone or something how many so called atheists admit to crying out to God for help. Wouldn't it be just great though if we could actually have a response to our prayer?

There are those, (and who am I to argue?) who claim to have actually heard a voice and claim too, this is the voice of God. I think however it is most unlikely for most of us to actually *hear* God speaking to us although there are a number of ways contact is made by Him. Recognising such takes time and patience, but if we persevere it does come.

First of all then, *when* do we pray? In fact, such a plan can be made to suit our own routine and preferences. Because God is present at all times and in every place we can really pray any time of the day or night. However, this very fact really gives scope for neglect or procrastination in prayer. There will be occasions maybe every day, when unexpectedly we need to have a quick, 'couple of words' prayer (Nehemiah 1 :4) and there is nothing wrong with this, on the contrary, it shows we recognise the immediate availability of our Best Friend. But treating God as a kind of Fire Brigade, used only in an emergency and then to be forgotten is not the way to establish a secure and ever growing relationship. We need to make a definite plan to set aside every day, some little time when, unhurriedly we can talk to God just about anything, sharing our fears and our joys, bringing to Him concerns about loved ones and friends in fact *absolutely anything* which may cross our minds and then take time just to be quiet and think about what we have said. Many people find some devotional reading is helpful at such a time and certainly I would recommend reading the Bible and then allowing time to meditate upon what has been read.

Circumstances will dictate when this quiet time can be fixed into one's daily routine. What may suit one could be unworkable to another. There are those who may arise in the morning perhaps fifteen minutes or so earlier. Again there are others who find that just before going to bed is better suited to them. *'In quietness and confidence shall be your strength.'* (Isaiah 30: 15) Most Christians find this to be true. If you are really serious in your quest of building a living relationship with God you must get this right, otherwise you will be in for a very rocky pathway.

Where do we pray? To the uninitiated, church is the most obvious place and of course, praying with others, maybe during a service does a great deal to develop our prayer life but this is only part of the answer. In the previous chapter we spoke about Jesus living in an atmosphere of prayer, this I believe should be our aim although it may be a goal which will never really be reached. Jesus certainly prayed in the Temple in Jerusalem and in the local Synagogues but this was only part of His prayer life as has already been mentioned. If it is possible we might be able to use a room in the home perhaps our bedroom. I have heard of at least one man who used his garden shed for this purpose! Why not! The first men to circle the moon testify to the reality of prayer out in space and the feeling that God was close by. Having worked 1200 feet below ground I certainly would state quite unequivocally that God so often came close to me and my prayers were just as real underground as they were on the surface.

Always start your prayers with thanksgiving. No matter how dark the picture, there is *always* something to thank God for.

I recall a little story about a minister in Cornwall a good many years ago, who was renowned for his prayers of thanksgiving – much to the annoyance I am afraid of one or two chapel folk. One very damp, foggy, miserable November morning, the smaller than usual congregation met for the service and discovered the heating had broken down which meant the building was almost like an ice box. The critics decided that at last, conditions were so bad that the minister just could not, surely, find anything to thank God for. As he stood to his feet to pray, he began, "O Lord! We thank Thee that every morning isn't as bad as this one..."

Seriously, a positive attitude in prayer will make all the difference. Just think for a moment about ones loved ones, or the provision of food and clothing, a roof over our heads, the gift of nature etc. You can see the list would be never ending, and thanking God in this way somehow puts 'things' into perspective and our minds are cleared of much of the unhelpful clutter we gather. Prayer moves our self centred world into a God centred one. Instead of seeing only the immediate tiny picture of life, we begin to see a much larger picture, viewing life as it were from God's point of view.

'Prayer gently lifts me to highest Heaven,
From earth's confusion to Jesus' breast;
My sin and weakness, my doubt and sorrow,
Are lost for ever in sweetest rest.'

Prayer has the ability of lifting us to a higher plain from that which surrounds us in this physical world. This is one of the purposes of prayer, it helps us see life with all complexities from a different view point and, whilst all the answers will not be forthcoming experience teaches that gradually, like pieces in a jigsaw puzzle, the whole picture begins to unfold bit by bit.

Patience is called for of course, there will be frustrations and on occasions we will be angry at the turn of events but we must not let these experiences sidetrack us into giving up. Share these thoughts too with God (even your anger) and you will be surprised how so often, into the mind there will come thoughts which can only come from God, and because we begin to see a much bigger picture will begin to make more sense than before. Certain situations may take a lifetime of patience and searching but it is worth it in the end.

Through prayer, we can often catch a glimpse, albeit a fleeting one, of the mind of God. This will not all come at once and we would be foolish to think it does or should. Even the disciples had to wait until the right time because their minds could not take in all what Jesus wanted to say to them. (John 16: 12) Paul spoke about seeing life with a blinkered vision and we will only see clearly when we reach Heaven (1 Cor. 13: 12)

We should not unduly concern ourselves because we cannot see (spiritually) too clearly all at once. We should avoid getting upset or downcast because we do not know the answer. If we are as diligent and faithful as we can be then, at the right time God will reveal the mystery.

One of the wonders of prayer is that it can so often benefit not only the one who is praying but the one being prayed for. In a remarkable way there is an invisible contact and the 'target' of the prayer so often becomes aware of this and feels an extra strength or help is available. This doesn't always happen and I cannot give a satisfactory explanation as to why this is so, but having been at the receiving end of prayer I certainly would testify to its benefits.

At this juncture, we are establishing the importance of prayer and we should guard this means of grace with every ounce of strength we can muster. There will be times when we just don't *feel* like praying. Don't let this put you off, indeed, it could well be that when you don't feel like praying is the very time you *must* pray. After all do we always *feel* like getting up in the morning and going to work? Does a child always *feel* like going to school? Of course not, but we do not allow our feelings to dictate our course of action, if we did, what a complete mess we would be in!

If prayer is the number one priority for an aspiring Christian, study of the Bible comes a close second. It is a constant source of bewilderment to me observing so many very clever, gifted men and women who have become experts in their chosen career and have spent many years of concentrated work and study to gain qualifications, yet cannot see the importance of spending time with God's word! Listening to a sermon may be all well and good and how refreshing it is to be able sit and listen to a servant of God expounding the Scriptures. We need to see however that the Sunday sermon is 'icing on the cake' rather than the only source of food. We need to feed our spirits on the other six days of the week – not just on a Sunday.

Knowledge of the Bible does not come automatically. It is hard work (although most enjoyable and rewarding), but there is no easy pathway to the knowledge it contains. It is called the *Word* of God and those who seek to know God will find He uses the Bible to speak directly to us. It follows therefore, if I do *not* spend time with the Bible I am closing my ears to the voice of God, and so will rob myself of that personal contact I am in fact seeking to nurture. On the other hand, if we do set aside, each day some time to read just a little of the Bible we will be amazed how often there is a message just for us.

Many, many Christians will testify that when reading, quite suddenly certain words or verses will suddenly appear almost to be printed in bold letters or illuminated and we discover such words are tailor made for us. They would also testify that one of the wonders of the Bible is its ability to disclose a message which we hadn't noticed before, or that a piece of Scripture reveals a new meaning even though that verse had been read many times before. This is very reassuring to the believer and he/she discovers this happens more and more as they become familiar with the Bible.

We need to be sensible when approaching study of this Book of books. I would not advise any one setting out upon the Christian pathway to read it from cover to cover. This would prove to be confusing and yes, I have to say even boring particularly with some of the early books. It would be such a pity to allow this to happen when it could be avoided with a little thought.

Obtaining a helpful daily reading guide is recommended – at least to begin with. Many churches have these printed and contain a day to day suggested portion of Scripture (a few verses) with helpful comments about such verses. Making a daily habit of reading then becomes an interesting, often exciting experience and one to be looked forward to eagerly. One will discover ones knowledge grows with words and verses somehow registering in the memory, to be called upon when needed. It takes time, but it is time well worth spending.

It is always a good thing, before commencing to read the Bible to have a prayer and ask God to help you understand and interpret what it is saying. If you have really saturated your mind with the life and teachings of Jesus you will find you will be interpreting Scripture in harmony with His spirit. This is the key which will open up the Bible to the believer. It may take some considerable time to place along side Christ's spirit with certain happenings recorded – particularly in the Old Testament, but do not allow this to deter you from reading. The truth will come if you keep searching.

Avoid, at all costs the dangerous practice some have of taking an isolated verse or chapter and suiting it to ones own situation. *All* Scripture is given by inspiration of God, (2 Tim. 3: 16) and to take an odd verse here and maybe one from there in order for us to prove a point or support a pet theory will not do us any good at all.

I was brought up on the King James version like so many of my peers but today there are so many modern interpretations which make Bible study so much more easily acceptable and understandable.

Attend a Bible class. A number of churches organise these and they are so helpful. If you feel really ambitious contact a Bible/ Theological college and take a course in Bible study.

There are so many ways you can improve your knowledge and it is all so very worth while. In time, you will develop your own particular way which is just right for you. You will also find that in just about every situation you can find yourself in, the Bible has an answer – if you look for it.

*****

It must be said that Christianity is a fellowship or family with God as our Father and believers as brothers and sisters. It follows then, as a family we meet together, and this is where the churches come in. In effect, churches are meeting rooms for believers, and come in all shapes and sizes. The type of meeting (service) too will differ from place to place. We can be sure there will be one which will suit our personality and in which we feel at ease and at home. I find this diversity of worship to be a great strength of Christianity rather than a stumbling block.

We are all quite different to one another. A quiet, formal approach may be just what some people want and they are drawn nearer to God in such an atmosphere. On the other hand, there are those who prefer a noisy, informal approach or a mixture of both. It really doesn't matter. We need to seek out the place in which we feel comfortable and happy and then support all we can.

There will be times when groups from all sides of the spectrum will meet or inter-change and at such times, there will be something which will enrich the true seeker after God, even from another fellowship.

President John F. Kennedy when giving one of his challenging speeches to the nation said something like this. *"Don't ask what can America can do for you, rather, ask what can you do for America."* This is the approach we too should have regarding our chosen church and our worship. I have heard all too often the statement, *"I didn't get anything out of the service."* Did they give anything to it? I think not! If we do not contribute to the spirit of our church we certainly will get very little, if anything out of it. What the church needs today perhaps more than ever before are men and women of stamina, who stay the course, stand their ground through good times as well as bad, and forever seek ways in which to contribute something helpful to its life. There are far too many Christians who, at the slightest disagreement will either change their allegiance and go to another church or stay away altogether.

I recall one lady who attended one of our Salvation Army corps many years ago. If she agreed with the officer then all was fine and you could count upon her 100% If you upset her though, she would remove her name patch from her uniform and stitch on the name tab of another nearby corps. The joke was that she had these name tabs on press studs to make it easier for her change them over. This had been going on for a good number of years. How sad.

To conclude this chapter, let me emphasise the importance of these three essential ingredients to building a secure relationship with the living God. Prayer – Bible study and Christian fellowship. There are other helps too but these head the list. To neglect any one of these is to court trouble and we will become victims of *daylight robbery.*

5. Whose fault is it anyway ?

I expect many will recall those childhood school days when the annual sports day was organised and our parents were invited to come along and watch. There was always the obstacle race with the children having to overcome certain problems before they could reach the winning line. Life is often described as a race and an obstacle race at that. And what obstacles!

There has been no attempt to hide the fact that when one embarks upon the race of life with God all will not be easy and straight forward. On the contrary, there will be times when we will feel absolutely everything is against us. Is it worth all the hassle?

It would be impossible to list every human problem which has contributed to the breaking point in the delicate relationship with God and faith has been severely dented if not shattered. Yet, with just a realistic and sensible approach to the problem, the outcome need not be as devastating as it often is.

A rather (and I have to say) *foolish* question many Christians ask, with some of these good folk having been a follower of Christ for many years is, "Why did this happen to me?" when faced with a problem be it in health, awkward people or whatever. If we analyse this question we would have to conclude that what they were really saying was, " Why did *God* allow this to happen?"

This same question is asked when there are happenings which are quite disastrous and innocent people are involved. It is a question asked when, as far as we can see, we have prayed a good prayer to benefit another yet the outcome has been quite the opposite to what we feel ought to have happened.

Often we think either God is not interested, or He is not listening, or He delights in being cruel or He is getting His own back ...

If this question ever features in our thinking then let us seek an answer. If we are afraid to put our faith under the microscope because we may not find the answer palatable then there is something very wrong with our faith. The ways of God may be very different to ours in some things and as we have already said He, who created Heaven and earth must of necessity be shrouded in mystery with certain aspects of His dealings forever being far beyond our understanding. Yet, having said this, He wants us to know Him and love Him and having been made in His image, (Gen. 1: 26 & 27) must see this includes the ability to *think for ourselves.* He is not afraid of being scrutinised with His dealings with mankind. The problem lies not in His compassion but in our lack of understanding. This becomes clearer to us as we patiently 'hang on' and trust despite all the questions.

I would like us to take a very careful look at problems which have attempted to rob me of that inner peace and which I think are common to most if not all people. To consider this objectively should not imply that my findings are the complete and final answer to the question asked since the beginning of time (if only!) They will be largely inconclusive but maybe help at the least get rid of some of the immature, foolish conclusions some people reach or are heading for.

First of all, the problem of sickness which can strike at random to any age, any race, any class, any creed. Rich or poor, wise or ignorant in fact any and every human being is susceptible. It is a condition which right thinking people would wish to avoid and it is obvious that God's plan for mankind includes good health. We can see this by the attitude Jesus had to those who were suffering any kind of health problem. So we ask a very big 'WHY?'

Before seeking an answer, are we sure of the question? I say this because the question which comes from the mouth in fact may not be the question really being asked in the heart.

Forgive a personal reference. At the onset of my own problems with health which led at last to a five week period of hospitalisation also being unable to continue working for a period of almost eighteen months. This in effect brought about early retirement and even as these words are being written, there is no real sign yet that I will ever regain the good health I once enjoyed.

I recall the large number of lovely folk who made the effort to visit me in hospital and in my home. They brought such joy and comfort to me. But, one or two expressed their dismay at seeing me in such a situation by using words something like, "It doesn't seem right that you should be suffering in this way." And some added the words, "after all you are such a good person." First of all I have to strongly disagree with their assessment of me being 'good'. If they really knew me they would not use such a word I assure you.

The inference though is quite clear. They were stating that it wasn't right for me, a Christian to suffer in this way and that God had let me down. In a strange way, they were trying to bring comfort to me but I really had to correct their thinking. To follow such a line of thought would lead them into stating that all Christians should escape sickness.

Now let us travel further down this pathway. Just imagine if this were to be true, what would be the outcome? Surely in a very short period of time every single person in this world would be Christian – and all for the wrong reason – to escape sickness.

This would then lead mankind into a life of recklessness, promiscuity, selfish self-gratification etc., because no matter how the body was to be abused, because he is a Christian, he would not suffer the consequences. What an absurd outlook we might say, yet this would be the natural consequences of going along such a pathway.

If I smoke, there is every possibility I may get lung cancer or some other disease of the lung. If I indulge in promiscuous sexual behaviour I could contract a sexually transmitted disease. If I am involved in a road, rail or air accident it is likely I will be hurt if not worse. Being a Christian really has nothing to do with the outcome of such behaviour. It can and does happen to anyone in any walk of life.

This consideration is applicable too in sicknesses which we have had no personal control over. There are so many viruses about these days which attack the system. Heredity problems which are a real burden for some families to carry. Food and water contamination, particularly with the travelling abroad which so many of us undertake these days.

To ask therefore, "Why has this happened?" is really a question which is quite unnecessary. We can see quite clearly why. And the real answer, given just a little thought will be applicable to so many other situations we come against too.

We can see, can we not, that to expect God, or any other agency to deliver us from such automatic consequences really is going beyond the realms of reason even though we may wish so desperately for healing..

Perhaps, from a personal point of view the aforementioned does carry our judgment – at least for some of the way, but how do we reconcile the suffering of innocent people. Those who have had no part to play in any happenings or relationships leading up to the tragedy? The most recent of these being the shattering incident of the terrorist attack upon the World Trade Centre twin towers in New York. Thousands of people, ordinary men, women and children lost their lives when the two planes were flown directly into the buildings.

This is one of the stark realities of evil. Having complete disregard for the dignity of human life, it inflicts pain, suffering and death on anyone – the more the better as far as it is concerned.

Since time began this has been the case. Think back to the World Wars. Think of Aberfan. Think of the Holy Land.

We all cry out "Why?" But in the cool light of day we can see why. Evil has the upper hand, controlling the minds of men and so they become instruments of the Devil. Such a statement is not given lightly or glibly. Whether we believe in a personalised Devil or not, no one can deny the existence of evil and that it does have the power to take over men's minds to such an extent they become blind to all expressions of goodness. A conflict between good and evil has always existed and we can be sure always will until the Last Day when evil will be defeated once and for all.

The *real* question we are asking surely is this. Why doesn't God intervene? If He is the all-kind, all-loving, all-powerful

God, how can He just sit back and do nothing when He sees such bad things happening?

Let me say at this point no one should feel guilty about asking such a question. It is one which every thinking Christian has asked at some time or other and to be fobbed off with some of the answers which have been given is an insult to us as well as to God. But there is no easy or slick answer. This age old problem needs to be very slowly approached with due thought and careful consideration otherwise we will find ourselves making excuses or apologising for God and this can *never* be right.

Let us take this step by step. In our heart of hearts we feel convinced that God is a *good* God. Have we any evidence for this? I think so. We read of Him stating that a sparrow, the most common of all birds does not fall to the ground without the knowledge of God. (Matthew 10:29) And that the very hairs on our head are all numbered. (Matthew 10: 30-31) Feeling sorry for the crowd He healed their sick and fed them. (Matthew 14 :14) He wept with those attending a funeral (John 11: 35) The Gospels are brim full of events involving Jesus with the lives of others where it is evident He has great love for the people and to see them in pain brought grief to Him. We need no further proof of course than the coming of Jesus into this world for, as John writes, *'God so loved the world that He gave His only Son..'* (John 3: 16)

Now, if all this is true, the suggestion that God takes delight in seeing people suffer, or is indifferent to their condition really is quite ludicrous. He would be a contradiction to Himself. But then to go further, as some people do, to actually blame Him and suggest He *sends* such suffering in order to punish us goes beyond comprehension. As far as I am concerned if this were to be true I would not want to associate myself one iota with Him. This is not a picture of the God which Jesus revealed when He came to earth.

Making this statement then we need to stand fast by it and make it the foundation stone upon which we build, for His love really is the key which will open the doors of our understanding.

Our suffering therefore is a result of infection or accident or violence or whatever. *It is not God oriented* and even though certain suffering may be through our own stupidity or downright sin, God does not choose to punish us in this way. It is a natural consequence of the wrong done to our body. We would be wise to remember this when trying to find a scapegoat to blame. We should keep in mind too that rather than finding actual pleasure in seeing us suffer, God has promised to be with us, supporting us in everyway. (Matt. 28: 20) If we need to be forgiven for abusing our body and this is the cause of our problems, and we in all sincerity ask Him to do this for us He will, without a shadow of a doubt. It may not bring healing to our physical suffering but it certainly will to our spirits.

There is another consideration in all this too. When I was a four year old child, I spent three months in hospital suffering from diphtheria. At that time, such a disease often proved fatal to children and I know my parents were at their wits end with worry.

Today we never hear about such an illness. In the western world it has virtually been eradicated, for which we are grateful I am sure. We could make a long list of complaints which are now part of medical history, and why? Research has brought about not just a cure but preventative steps to make it impossible for such germs to take hold in the slightest way.

Of course other illnesses have taken their place, such as cancer, aids, dementia etc. I have no doubt that in due time – and I think sooner rather than later – these too will take their place in the history books to be replaced by others.

Mankind has been able to effect cures to what have been known as fatal illnesses *despite* having all the draw-backs and restrictions of a sinful world being led by the same spirit and desire to bring full health which Jesus had. Just imagine if you can, what progress there would have been had there been no such restrictions!

Think for one moment the cost involved in research for cancer and the advancement being already made and compare it with the cost of the few weeks war against the terrorists in Afghanistan! If all the money and brain spent upon weapons of destruction had been channelled into *healing,* where would medical science be today? It makes you think!

This is yet another way in which evil stunts the growth of humanity, taking him far from the person God intended him to be.

There is yet another thought we might like to consider as we attempt to take a panoramic view of this age-old mystery, and looking at the situation from yet another angle will be another way of coping in a dignified and optimistic way.

If we Christians take seriously the promise of Jesus that He has prepared a place for those who believe in Him when this life is over, we will not attach undue importance to this life.

This is not to suggest our lives are to be regarded as worthless and not worth living. Life is precious and particularly so when shared with those we love and who love us. There are so many, many blessings we enjoy to make life a happy experience, although not every person is so blest.

Jesus said that we must not be afraid of those who can kill *only* our bodies – but cannot touch our souls. (Matt. 10: 28) He also spoke about not being worried about what we eat or drink or what we are to wear, but rather to seek to do God's will. (Matt. 6: 31-32) Surely what He is saying is get your priorities right. If we see only this life as the be all and end all of things then we cannot help but fall into the trap of hanging on, at all costs to what we have around us.

If on the other hand, we take Him at His word and link this to our deepest instinct, we will view life just as a temporary sojourn and look forward to a more fulfilling life with Him. Paul echoes this when he states that, *'Bodily exercise is all right, but spiritual exercise is much more important and is a tonic for all you do………'* (1 Tim. 4:7-10)

In Palestine, at the time of Jesus there were multitudes of people suffering all types of sicknesses but only very, very few were healed. Is this to imply Jesus couldn't care less about this vast crowd, if not, why didn't they receive healing from His hand?

In the book of John we read that the followers of Jesus will do greater miracles than those which He had performed. (John 14: 12-13) Compare if we like Jesus miraculously giving one blind man back his sight (Mark 10: 46-52) to the amazing on-going healing of blindness in parts of Africa where thousands of people, not just one man, can now see again. We do not pour cold water upon the miracle Jesus performed but rather see that His followers have interpreted His words (and rightly so) to follow his example and attitude towards healing. What He said and did is now the responsibility of those of us who call ourselves by His name.

There are those of course who strongly suggest that if we are not healed after praying about it, the fault is in *our* faith rather than in the love of God. This to me is not a satisfactory response to this problem. Some of the 'giants' of faith have suffered the most prolonged and agonising illnesses. We need to dismiss such thoughts from our minds for it only adds to our burden.

A well known fact is that there are people alive today, and living normal, healthy lives who, at some time were diagnosed with a terminal illness.

On the other hand, there are just as many people who ought to be alive today but just gave up and, despite all the best care the medical profession could give them it was of little use. How do we reconcile these two opposing corners?

I recall one of my school teachers who, from time to time would write on the blackboard texts or proverbs, hoping her little 'angels' would absorb them into the mind and make them better people. One such proverb read, *'As a man thinketh, so is he.'*

The mind, that illusive control panel situated deep within the brain and somehow invisibly connected to the heart does have a very powerful and dominant place over the body. And somewhere in this same place there lodges the spirit and soul of a person. The conscience is housed in an adjoining room and all unite to dictate what, where and when the body will respond to any given situation. We have all heard of people who made up their minds they will *not* get better from their illness even though they should and could – and they don't.

So where does faith or the lack of it come into place? Are we to assume faith plays no part in healing but it is rather what we might call 'auto-suggestion'?

I think both are part of the same answer. The mind is active – it has to be – to trigger off our faith. *Belief* is the first rung on the ladder quickly followed by *faith,* although it has to be said there are times when our faith is not fully realised. When people came to Jesus for healing, he often would challenge them as in the incident with the crippled man at the Pool of Bethesda. (John 5: 6) What was man *thinking* first of all, then the act of faith in his healing. It is worth noticing that so often Jesus would include words that the recipient should 'sin no more.'

Attitude of mind can and so often does have a bearing upon our physical condition – not always – but quite often. If we are not healed, this does not necessarily mean our faith is lacking but rather is an indication we need to re-direct it. After all, what is even more important than healing is the fulfilment of His promise that He will be with us, no matter what. If we really believe this, it is rewarded by a contented faith which is unshakable.

I would take a further step, and run the danger of many people either disagreeing with me strongly or at least not understanding when I say when all is said and done, the one real prayer we should say, the *only* request we need to make is asking for His presence. With this, we need nothing else!

The beautiful old hymn written by Henry Francis Lyte and sung at Wembley at Cup finals (for a reason I do not know) echoes this very thought. Indeed, he commences and then completes his hymn with the same words, *'Abide with me.'* He does not list every experience of life but rather concentrates upon the days facing death nevertheless, such a prayer is applicable from birth to death (and beyond).

However, comparatively few people have reached this point in their prayer life so we need to tackle, where possible life's problems as they arrive.

I once heard an eminent medical practitioner state whilst taking part in a discussion on T.V., that doctors' do not bring healing! He went on to say, the person's own body does the healing, having the ability to deal with so many different kinds of injuries and germs with no outside help whatsoever. Where a doctor comes in is when the germ or injury is too big for the body's own 'repair system' to heal. The doctor *assists* in so many ways the natural processes the body will bring in to play.

A person's mind is all part of this healing process, if we *think* positively this is a terrific ally to the healing work. Over my long life and with the necessity of moving frequently due to my work, I have needed to register with a different doctor in various towns and villages. There are those who stand out well for having the ability of saying just the right thing and in the right way to ensure I do not despair but rather keep positive.

There have been those on the other hand who have made me feel worse when leaving the surgery than I was when I entered!

When Jesus spoke to those people who were searching for healing, He had the ability to cause His 'patients' to think positively, and this surely helped in their healing.

We can answer so many of our own prayers for healing by a sensible approach to our way of life. The way we are living may be causing health problems and we may not see that what we really need isn't medicine but a turnaround in our lifestyle.

However when, despite all our positive thinking and the best possible treatment there is still further deterioration and the eventual cessation of life, what can we do? When, although we may believe God does have the power to heal yet, for some unknown reason this does not happen, where do we go from here?

I would suggest that the strength of our relationship with Him will help us accept the situation as it is, and cradled in His loving embrace take whatever life has in store for us. Whether we have faith in God or not, the conditions will not be changed with struggles or bitterness of spirit. If we see a more fulfilling life ahead, where all pain and suffering is at an end, where wrongs are put right and love, justice and tranquillity are the norm, what a happy person we will be, even in our last moments of life. We *can* have this assurance!

'I'm in His hands, I'm in His hands,
Whate'er the future holds, I'm in His hands.
The days I cannot see, have all be planned for me,
His way is best you see, I'm in His hands.'

6. The trouble with people is...

If the problem of sickness has featured high in my thinking giving me cause to question God, I think the behaviour and attitude of fellow Christians must come only a little lower down the scale. To observe the lives of a number of people who claim to be Christians just shocks and bewilders me.

I think, as a young person growing up in a Salvation Army corps in Yorkshire I was blissfully unaware of any problem within the fellowship of the Corps. Subsequent experience has taught me that it is human nature to have differences of opinion even downright arguments and falling out with each other. This happens whether there be two or two hundred people.

Now different ideas and thoughts amongst a congregation is to be encouraged and brings freshness and variety to the ministry of the church. If we cannot cope with a person who has a different view point to the one we hold this only reveals our own insecurity. One of the attractions of a Bible class or a church members meeting is this inter-change of thoughts and ideas, and if we are sensible, will widen and enrich our knowledge.

Yet there are members who appear to take such delight in causing problems and unpleasantness, and to a leader can be a real thorn in the flesh. More often than not, the disagreement is over some very silly, minor sort of thing, yet such people are like a dog with a bone and will not let go or see the others' point of view.

Facing problems *outside* the church we may be able to cope with quite well and easily – indeed – they often sharpen our wits and quicken our dedication. But having to face these from those *inside* the church is another matter. When Jesus set about choosing the twelve disciples he saw in each of them, the possibility, the potential of leadership of the church in each and every one of them, and this included Judas Iscariot. What ever his motive behind Judas's betrayal, I am convinced it was the very fact this came from one of His *inner* group of friends which caused the most heart ache to Jesus.

I regrettably have to state, and find no pleasure in this, that the worse things I have had said or done to me have come not from those 'sinners' out there, but from the 'saints' inside who wear a similar uniform to that which I wear. And we must not be mistaken into thinking this only happens within the Army. My conversation with so many ministers of other churches confirms they also are similarly plagued. This should not be, but it is true. I firmly believe it the biggest problem the church has to face regarding any lack of progress - its own people. Ghandi stated the thing which stopped him from becoming a Christian were the Christians themselves!

The tragedy is that such folk, who are often used by the Devil can be the cause of shaking our own love and dedication to the church and even to God. They can say or do things which we know are downright unchristian and, catching us at a low ebb we can respond in like manner and we can then be robbed of a happy productive church life.

What do we do? Well we cannot close our eyes and pretend they are not there, but we need to be alert to the real possibility of being dragged down by them.

Often, the problem can be dealt with successfully and amicably if this is tackled in a loving, yet firm way. Talking things over in a friendly fashion can work wonders and may actually reveal a cry for help. *Our* reaction could well determine the outcome. Waving the big stick really is not the best solution. The Bible states that, *'a soft answer turns away wrath.'* (Proverbs 15: 1) Doing one's best to diffuse an otherwise explosive situation calls for real diplomacy but when this works, how rewarding it is. Jesus said in His '*Sermon on the Mount'* that the best way to deal with those who are against us is to love them. (Matthew 5: 43-45) It would be foolish to suggest this is an easy course to take, particularly when we are not to blame for the problem, but it is the course Jesus suggests – and it works. This does not mean we necessarily have to *like* them! But Christian love desires the best for every person, even those bent upon causing trouble. Our love for them therefore will seek the best, even for such folk and you know, after a while we might be surprised to discover our dislike of that person gradually disappears.

One of the problems unfortunately is that some of us have a very short fuse and we can, at the slightest suggestion of opposition or disagreement 'blow our top' and then regret this afterwards. This usually means we are placed in the position of apologising when, with just a little bit of self control it can all be avoided. Paul speaks about the Christian, living a life which is not easily ruffled or provoked, (1 Cor. 13: 5) Many an upset could so easily be avoided if our response is controlled.

Thinking positively about our adversary is so helpful in this. We do not need to be a clever psychologist to see that there usually is an underlying problem worrying our opposite number, hence their unchristian reaction. Meeting fire with fire will only cause the flame to burn higher. Our gentle understanding and patience can so often be like pouring cool waters upon the fire and bring about a change in attitude. Whatever the other person may be like they are still part of the family of God and as such is our brother or sister in Christ.

If the upset is not resolved we cannot make this an excuse for us slackening in our devotion to God or our church. We cannot blame them if we loose our faith for, in the final analysis we are responsible for our own salvation. (Phil. 2:12) and no one can pluck us out of the hand of God. (John 10: 29) The only person who can take us away from God is our own self!

Every effort should be made therefore to live at peace with all men (Hebrews 12: 14) and where this really is impossible, when our offer of friendship and handshake are rejected by the other party, this must not adversely affect *our* devotion to God. Just remember we have been bought with a great price – nothing less than the life's blood of our Lord Jesus Christ. To allow such a silly reason as a disagreement to turn us from Him is to belittle what He has done for us. When it comes to the crunch, why should we allow such a thing to steal away from us the greatest treasure we could ever possess? This would be worse than daylight robbery – and of all people – we would be the losers.

Winston Churchill made many memorable speeches and used sentences and phrases which are now in common usage. When commenting about conflict between nations he declared, *"We want jaw, jaw not war, war."* Rather than being the last resort – and no matter how bitter the conflict, to solve the issue there must be talk. After many, many years of war nations eventually have had to come to the negotiating table and sort their differences out. How much better to do this *first* and so avoid a collision course. We need to remember too that the Spirit of God will assist and guide us in the way we should go.

It would be superfluous to suggest how we might tackle opposition from *outside* the church, because if we really are living a Christ-like life, this is what we must expect. (Matt. 5: 11-12) It has been said we should only have cause to worry if we *do not* have opposition, it would mean we are failing in our witness! Sufficient to say if we live close to our Lord, He will lead us through such trials and we will witness so often our opposes becoming our allies when our approach has been in the spirit of our Lord.

*****

There are occasions however when we feel the opposition comes from the 'establishment' and we might feel completely inadequate to meet the challenge. This may come from local leadership in our church, or have more far reaching implications affecting a much larger area, even nation or world wide.

We need to see the difference between the *doctrine* or the fundamental *beliefs* of the church to the *programme* and *discipline* it embodies. There is a difference, a very real difference and we need to see this.

If the church leaders are tinkering around with the Articles of Faith we need to defend this with every ounce of energy we can possess and this is best done *within* the church rather than leaving it and criticising it from outside. I think however, this is most unlikely to happen and it is rather the programme or the applied disciplines of the church which we fall out with.

As a life long member of The Salvation Army of course there have been decisions made, directives sent out, orders and regulations given from 'up there' which I, along with many others have totally disagreed with, and I have not been slow to let my feelings known, albeit in a Christian manner. But to take personal offence, to give up being a Salvationist, even being a Christian really is a too severe a course of action to take – but so many have taken this way.

Taking time to think the matter through is so very important if we are to avoid becoming a casualty in this matter and so walk into the open arms of our adversary.

First of all, let us remind ourselves of our early days in the Faith. Remember when we first came into a knowledge of Jesus Christ as Saviour and Lord. Recall the great joy of being freed from the weight of sin and the feeling of elation as we began this new life with the living God.

Bring to mind the warm helpful fellowship of those fellow believers. Recall the enjoyable services, the thrill of becoming an active member of our chosen church. Now, did we make an almighty mistake, were we fooled in someway when all this took place? Was it all emotion? Had we just followed the crowd like sheep?

In all honesty, there may be a few who would answer in the affirmative. Most of us would say however that our experience was real and personal and brought us such joy and that we wish we could return to such days.

The decision to 'pack it all in' in most cases is not really a sudden one. It could well be that over a long period of time certain happenings have hurt or disappointed us. We needed support and it wasn't forthcoming and now we have reached that last final straw which has broken the proverbial camel's back. I suggest what might be missing in our religious experience is a vision of what *could* be. Let me explain.

Take for an example a gardener who moves house and discovers the garden he now possesses has not been touched for years and is just a place for rubbish and weeds. He could despair because all he can see is a place of neglect, yet in his mind he has *the vision* of what it can become. It may take some years of hard work to realise the vision but he works at it, despite the setbacks he encounters on the way.

Or take a skinny eight stone weakling who joins a gym. All he can see by looking into the mirror is a 'bag of bones' and looking around the gym is embarrassed by the presence of men who have good muscular physiques. What does he do? Pack it up as bad job? Not if he has any backbone at all. No, he has in his mind *a vision* of what he might become with real dedication and hard work. Maybe another Mr. Universe? He may never fully realise his vision but this does not deter.

This principle is also applicable when considering our own Christian living and our church too. Don't dwell upon the 'now' but have a *vision* of what we and our church can become in the fullness of time.

Jesus is our prime example in this, first of all with people. We are told that He knew all men. (John 2: 24 & 25) He was aware therefore of man's weaknesses as well as his strengths, yet this did not deter Him from choosing twelve ordinary, working-class men to be given the responsibility of handling the Gospel and becoming the founders of the Church. Taking just one individual to illustrate this we look at Peter, who was I suppose the number one of the group. Peter was the spokesperson for them, often opening his mouth when he ought to have kept it shut! He was so full of brave words, and declared even if all the others fail, Jesus could depend upon him (Matt. 26: 33-35). Jesus knew Peter's faults but this did not stop Him from stating that Peter was to be the Rock upon which He would build the Church (Matt. 16: 18)

The Lord could see what Peter *was* at that moment of time but He had a vision of what Peter *could become.* I would suggest this was the way in which Jesus viewed everyone He met. Not just what they *were,* but what they *could be.* Just think about ourselves for a moment or two and we cannot help but agree.

This is an important lesson all Christians should endeavour to learn when they come to the point of washing their hands of those who cause problems and throwing in the proverbial towel. Remember, what God has done for us, He can do for them. We have to catch the same vision for them which Jesus possesses and do all in our power to create the conditions to realise this vision.

Remember too that the church is made up of people who will be at various stages in their religious experience. There will be those who are real saints and maybe have been travelling along the Christian pathway for years. Others may still be babies in Christ and so will need a lot of help and understanding.

These are the kind of people who make up the Church. Ordinary folk with hopes and fears, joys and sorrows, aspirations and despairs. In other words, people like you and me! What a revelation! Is there any need to say more?

But the individuals become a group and out of that group there emerges people who become leaders and make decisions for the church. Some rise to very high offices and wield a great deal of influence. It is when decisions are made which we might disagree with that we can find ourselves at variance with 'the church'.

Remember, no matter how high in its ranks an individual might rise they are still *people.* Experience and the guiding support of those around them will be helpful but mistakes can and are still made. No one is infallible!

Let us therefore apply this 'vision principle' to our church, no matter what denomination this might be.

Think of all the very best attributes such an organisation can possess, e.g. spirit filled; loving; caring; onward-going; pure; etc., etc. Now this is the vision we must keep in our minds at all times and must do our part in working toward its fulfilment. So what if others do not share this vision? It makes no difference. So we are let down and disappointed? Of course we are, but it still makes no difference. The vision needs to remain clear in our minds and be the set target of the heart.

In the book of Proverbs, the Bible speaks about people who have no vision perishing. (Proverbs 29: 18) The more one thinks about this the more one can see this to be true.

During the days of the prophets of Israel and at a particularly bad time for that nation, Ezekiel had a vision. In this vision he saw a valley of dry bones which God said could live again and become a great army. (Ezekiel 37: 1-14) Ezekiel never saw this happen but this did not adversely affect the vision at all.

Surely one of the best examples we can have is that of our Lord Jesus Himself and His attitude toward the Temple in Jerusalem, which was the Jewish equivalent to a cathedral.

We recall how this holy place had been turned into a market place. Its original purpose being almost lost and allowed to degenerate into a robber's paradise. (Mark 11: 15-17) This was one of the few occasions we read of Jesus becoming angry. He loved the Temple and saw what it ought to be, a house of prayer (Isaiah 56: 7) yet with the blessing of the priests it had become a den of robbers (Jer: 7: 11)

This fact though did not dim the vision Jesus had for the Temple, nor did it take away any love He had for the place. We read it was His custom to attend a place of worship every Sabbath (our Sunday) (Luke 4: 16) and nothing and no one would prevent Him from attending.

He didn't condone the wrong, but would not allow someone else's failings to interfere with His time of worship.

When Paul was on trial before king Agrippa, he told of his meeting with Jesus on the Damascus road which led to the commission Jesus gave him to preach the gospel. Paul stated that, 'he was not disobedient to the heavenly *vision,'* and neither must we nor any follower of Christ.

Included in *our* vision is meeting the Lord, face to face when we move from this world to the next. We must not allow *anything* or *anyone* to stand in our way for, if we do, it will be the greatest triumph for Satan as he views the spoils of his theft, rubbing his hands together with the greatest of glee. The Great Train Robbery pales into insignificance in comparison!

There is an additional consideration too regarding the thoughts we may have of giving in. Despite all its faults and failings, the Church has been the instrument God has chosen to be the custodians of the Gospel. History records the many occasions when an attempt has been made by some, either by accident or design to tamper with the Truth and for a while appear to succeed. But the Spirit of God, active as He is, in a miraculous way brings His people back to the genuine Truth. There has been and always will be people who are ultra sensitive to the promptings of God's Spirit and so ensure that in the end, even after persecution, the Word of God stands as it should – *firm.*

This very fact surely should encourage us to stand firm too. It could well be He is depending upon us to protect His truths and if we fail Him, what sadness would we bring to His own heart?

We must not underestimate our influence either upon those other members of our fellowship who may hold us in high esteem and an example of what a Christian really is. It is an awesome responsibility but it is true, there are those who look up to us and so just imagine the shock and disappointment which would come to them if we gave up? It could be the cause for their withdrawal too.

Earlier in this book I spoke about the church needing people of real stamina and not jelly fish with no backbone. Being able to resist the Devil, no matter where he strikes or who he chooses to deliver the blow, is the responsibility of every Christian.

'If all were easy, if all were bright,
Where would the cross be, and where the fight?
But in the hardness, God gives to you
Chances of proving that you are true.'

In the very early days of our discipleship, we were left in no doubt that we cannot and must not expect an easy pathway. If we couldn't stand the heat we ought to have got off the stove long before now!

My advice to any possible casualty in this holy war is to spend some time, in real quietness and away from the demands of life in prayer. Seek God's guidance upon the course of action to be taken. It could well be that we are at such a low ebb because through one reason or another we have neglected that essential daily contact with our Lord and so have become vulnerable to this onslaught by the devil.

Don't leave your church. Don't lay down your arms. Fight it through and you will emerge from this experience a stronger and wiser person and you will have foiled the Devil's plan to steal God's precious gift to you.

'WHO is on the Lord's side?
Who will serve the King?
Who will be His helpers other lives to bring?
Who will leave the world's side?
Who will face the foe?
Who is on the Lord's side? Who for Him will go?'

7. A Wild Goose Chase?

In chapter 4 under the title 'Bricks & Mortar' amongst other things the study of the Bible was listed as a priority if the new Christian is going to grow. This cannot be emphasised too often or too strongly. I expect many Christians wish, when confronted by callers at their door who quote various texts to support their story that they had a greater knowledge of the Bible – if only to put the callers right!

It has already been said this knowledge does not come automatically, neither does it come all at once. It takes many years of patient study – on a day to day basis – to acquire such knowledge.

It will be discovered however that there are some parts of the Bible which are difficult to understand. Certain verses and chapters can be interpreted in a number of ways and this can be quite confusing.

When Philip met up with the Ethiopian nobleman he discovered he was reading from what we call the Old Testament. However he admitted he didn't understand fully what the words really meant and asked Philip to help him. (Acts 8: 26-40) This he did and the Ethiopian went happily on his way.

The Bible should never, ever be read without first asking God to help understand its true meaning. This prayer is so often answered directly to our minds and how glad we are this does happen. On other occasions however God uses another agency to clarify His Word. This may be through a book or a person or in some other way.

The problem however of such an interpretation coming through another person is that it will, inevitably have some of that person's outlook and experience colouring the answer. It does mean therefore that even when we have received from another their interpretation, it could well be this is only partially correct *for us.* We must still be alert to the promptings of God's Spirit who will make any necessary corrections when we are able to accept them. The words I have written in this book and which are being read now come into this same category. I dare not claim that what I have written is the complete and absolute revelation from God!

When we interpret Scripture in the spirit of Jesus, we will most likely have questions about a number of incidents too. Not that this should put us off studying, but it is fact we need to keep at the back of our mind. We must not feel guilty either about having such questions. As I have said before, God isn't afraid of being scrutinised and if we diligently seek we will in due time find. (Luke 11: 9)

I am saying all this because, as followers now of Christ we will naturally want to do what is pleasing to Him. The Bible is one of the main sources of direction a Christian can take. It has been said that the Bible can be likened to a map showing us the way with Jesus as the compass, to set the map straight. He does not send us out on a wild goose chase. What He asks of us, through His grace is attainable. If this were not so what would be the point in trying?

When the rich, young ruler came to Jesus seeking the right way to live (Matt. 19: 16) Jesus pointed to the Ten Commandments. (Matt. 19: 18) This was a natural response from the Lord because the Jews were brought up to keep the Law of Moses which included these very same commandments. It is interesting to note that subsequent verses indicate that although the man had kept these laws (in his eyes at any rate) he was aware there was still something missing and he believed Jesus had the answer. On another occasion, Jesus summed up the whole of the Old Testament laws by stating loving God and people is the key to success (Matt. 22: 34-40) Our relationship with God, as it develops becomes a loving one, and rather than trying to avoid sinning or breaking the law in order to escape punishment, we seek to please Him because we love, rather than fear Him. It is our personal responsibility to seek His will for us and then give ourselves completely to this task.

The key word I am sure you will have already detected is *love.* If any relationship in this life is of any value be it man and wife, child and parent or a friendship between two people, there is an affection one for another and I am not speaking about some unnatural relationship. Whether some would go as far as to say they might actually *love* another person due to its present day connotations is questionable but one cannot deny there is some kind of feeling, one for another and each will seek to benefit the other in various ways and certainly avoid at all costs causing harm or upset deliberately.

It is just the same with our growing relationship with Jesus Christ although we do not hide the fact that we love Him with an ever growing love.

Out of our love then we seek to please Him by doing what He wants us to do and in so doing we find yet more joy and fulfilment than ever.

Yet certain texts *may* at first sight appear to make demands which are not only unreasonable but unattainable too. This then makes our desire to show our love a burdensome chore and robs us of the very joy He has promised (John 15: 11) and despite the fact that He spoke about His yoke, (following Him) being an easy one. (Matt. 11: 29-30) Either He contradicts Himself or the questionable texts have not been fully understood or incorrectly interpreted.

Take for example the many references in the New Testament to '*the fruit*' of the Christian. Paul interprets this (and I agree with him) as the outward evidence in the *character* of a believer to the change which has taken place within, and includes love, joy, peace etc. (Galatians 5: 22) Yet quite recently I heard one preacher enthusiastically and with authority declare that "As the fruit of an apple tree is an apple and the fruit of a pear tree is a pear, so the fruit of a Christian is another Christian!" In other words, if we, as followers of Christ do not give evidence of this by making *new* Christians then we are failures as Christians.

Now we really must avoid this kind of thinking because it is as dangerous as its is wrong. You can take absolutely *every* reference to 'the fruit' contained in the New Testament and keeping it in its original setting we discover it never ever applies to making new Christians.

Of course it is wonderful to feel we have been instrumental in bringing a person near to Christ. At the conclusion of every Salvation Army meeting there is an invitation to members of the congregation to make a decision for Christ and to signify this by making their way to the front of the Hall to kneel at the Mercy Seat. What officer has not shed tears of joy when there has been this visible response to such an invitation? And how often are we exhorted to make this our aim?

Yet what about those times when there is *no* response? Does it mean the preacher has been unfaithful in some way to his calling? What about the person who is ministering in a situation which is notoriously hard and difficult. Is he less a Christian because he is not like the minister in the next church which is full of helpful people and is making new members all the time? I think not. At the age of fifteen years I commenced 'pub-booming' (this term is used to describe Salvationists who sell *'The War Cry'* in public houses.) In my early days, often men would say to me, "Do you save women?" naively I responded with a nod of the head and a definite "Yes!" At which the man would respond by asking me to save him one for next Saturday night!

I soon learned how to answer, but in truth my response should have been a resounding 'No' because I can't save anyone, only God can do that. The first sermon preached on the very day the Church was born was given by Peter. We read that three thousand people were added to their number (Acts 2: 41) In verse 47 we read, '*And the Lord added to their number daily those who were being saved.*' Peter fearlessly gave the message but it was the Lord who did the converting. (See also 1 Cor. 3: 4-8) We need to remember this at all costs.

This fact does not give licence for laziness or a couldn't care less attitude. We must do all in our power to persuade people to commit their lives to Christ and create as far as we can conditions which will be conducive to such a decision. In the end though, no matter how much we plead or how many tears are shed, *it is Christ who does the converting.*

Don't be tempted to take on more than God intends for you. In this day when looking for results appear to be the norm we can so easily think if *we* do not have converts we are failures. We are not!

The *Fruit of the Christian* is listed in the book of Galatians and has already been referred to. The full list reads as follows. *'The fruit of the Spirit is love, joy, peace, patience, kindness, goodness, faithfulness, gentleness and self-control.'* (Gal. 5: 22-23) If Christians concentrate upon this fruit, then according to our faithful living, the Lord will add to the church those He will. People will take more notice of a genuine person who may not *shout* aloud his beliefs rather than someone who is all noise but whose character leaves a lot to be desired.

In our desire to follow Christ and the quest to do all that is required, the statement found in the *Sermon on the Mount* has caused and still causes many aspiring Christians to shake their heads in dismay and feel such a way is not for them after all. I refer to the words of Jesus when He states that we are to *'... be perfect as God is perfect.'* (Matt. 5: 48)

Like so many, I have heard preachers wax long and hot about perfection in God's eyes, and rather than the sermon lifting me up, I have come away – not quite suicidal – but certainly very depressed because I knew I could never ever reach such a standard. But is God expecting and commanding that suddenly we change from a person who is prone to errors and mistakes and even sin, to one who becomes almost an angel? Surely not.

The whole of chapter 5 of the book of Matthew is well worth reading, as are the following two chapters which make up the sermon of Jesus. The verses preceding the command to be perfect deal with our attitude to others, not only those we like and get on with but those too who we would find it difficult to call friends. According to Jesus there must be no difference in the way we deal with people from either side. We must be completely generous as well as impartial. In *this* way, we are copying God's dealings with all men and so become faultless or *perfect* like Him.

When a gardener observes a growing plant, he does so at every stage of its growth. We might ask, 'when does a plant reach perfection?' Immediately most would look forward to the time when the flower has appeared or the vegetable is ready for the table. Yet seriously, even before the seed has actually germinated, are we not looking at something which is already perfect? When the first shoots are observed, although only a very young plant it is still perfect. And so on through the various stages of its growth and the days, weeks and months it takes in growing.

Like the plant, although there is a final perfection we are working for, if we are at our best en-route to this, then no matter how immature we might be we are in a sense perfect? A newly born baby is perfect yet he/she is far from reaching the potential which growth will bring.

In other words, we must not mistake perfection as meaning full maturity. In the spiritual sense it means we are the best as we can be *at that point* in our lives.

Absolute and complete perfection will only come when we have moved out of this poor old world into the promised land Jesus has prepared for us (John 14: 2) and we must aim for this. Until this happens though, live with Jesus, follow Him as closely as you can, accept the 'light' you have been given and you will see, as will others, the real fruit of the spirit taking over and your prayer to 'Be like Jesus' will gradually come true.

The word *holy* is not dissimilar to the word *perfect* in its application to aspiring Christians. In my dictionary, the word *holy* means; sacred, set apart for the service of God, high spiritual excellence.

To a follower of Christ this is a description of a Christian. There is no special week, day or hour which is any more sacred than others. A *real* follower sees *every moment of every day* as sacred and no matter where they might be and engaged in whatever activity, they are not released from the responsibilities of being a Christian. There is no such thing as a 'Sunday go to meeting Christian'.

We are set apart as living vessels every moment of our life to be used by Him to bring Him glory and honour.

'All my days and all my hours,
All my will and all my powers,
All the passion of my soul,
Not a fragment, but the whole
Shall be Thine dear Lord.'

A truly *holy* person will display the fruit of the spirit not in an arrogant way, but in a way as to make his observers think of God. He doesn't seek his own praise but the glory of God.

No, it isn't going to be easy but nothing really worthwhile ever is when you come to think of it. Avoid falling into the trap of demanding more from your performance as a follower of Christ than He does. He came to bring you more *abundant life* and certainly not to put a weight around your neck. Keeping this in mind will release you from untold pressure and bring liberty and freedom to really *enjoy* His presence. God's close and continuing presence and help will ensure this.

It goes without saying there will be times of disappointment and we will fail, but never despair. Share these times with Jesus and He will lift you up again to continue your journey.

Once again you will have had a victory over the Devil and stopped him in his tracks even before he could rob you.

8. Handpicked

'I think, when I read that sweet story of old,
When Jesus was here among men,
How He called little children as lambs to His fold,
I should like to have been with them then.
I wish that His hands had been placed on my head,
That His arm had been thrown around me,
And that I might have seen His kind look when He said:
Let the little ones come unto Me!'

I would expect most Christians will, at some time or other find themselves wishing, like the writer of the above verse, they could have actually been present when Jesus walked the earth as a man. I know I have!

Just think what confusion would have been saved with some of the statements accredited to Him in the New Testament? The words written about His life relied upon the memories of the people who knew Him – and this, many years later. Whilst I have no problem accepting the essential truths have been recorded, there are some statements which appear to be just the skeleton or outline of His words. I would like to have more 'flesh' put on to the 'bones.' We all know how easy it is for two people to be told the same story yet when asked to repeat the story later, differ quite dramatically from the original and from each other. Hence the occasional confusion.

Having said this though, in a remarkable way God, through His Spirit has led His children into the truth, and He still does. But it is no easy matter.

I hope we have established that being a Christian is concerned with a growing relationship with the living God rather than keeping a set of rules. If this relationship is truly and sincerely developed, then we help clear the way for direct communication with the Lord, and He reveals His will to us.

Seeking to please Him and do what He wants us to do has already been spoken about in previous pages. It is established I hope in our heart and mind that the most important response we can make is by living a life which is blessed by the fruit of the spirit. But it doesn't end there.

By nurturing the relationship which is on a day-to-day basis, the Christian becomes more and more sensitive to the promptings of God. Many will testify to being led directly into a situation by Him. How often the name of a person will, as it were out of nowhere suddenly feature in the mind, and when contact is made with that person it is obvious they were just waiting for us. Maybe during our prayer time this has happened and what a thrill this brings to us. The wonderful thing is that the more we respond positively to such Divine prompting the more this happens.

Yet this is not the end by any means. For whilst living a spirit led life is so rewarding and fulfilling for us, and acceptable and pleasing to God, He has yet more surprises in store.

The words of Jesus as found in the book of Matthew can be interpreted in a number of ways. *'Many are called but few are chosen'* Matt. 22: 14) It could mean many people are called to be Christians but few choose to accept. It could mean many are called to follow Christ but only a few are chosen to become His ministers. Again it could mean many are called to become His disciples but few are chosen to enter Heaven. I have heard sermons with each of these interpretations used as the theme for the words uttered. There are other interpretations. I wish I could have asked Jesus what He really meant.

We believe in the Priesthood of all believers. That is, every man, woman and child who call themselves Christians have been ordained by God to represent Him to the world. No person can escape this privilege and responsibility. If you are a Christian you become the instrument of grace in God's plan to reconcile the world to Himself.

Bringing honour and glory to God in every aspect of our life is paramount, and to take part or be involved in anything which does not fulfil this purpose is, to the say the least, questionable.

It means our daily employment must fulfil this purpose too. There are so many men and women who find themselves working at monotonous and repetitive duties in order to 'earn a crust,' but this does not excuse the Christian of their responsibility to complete the task faithfully and honourably which in itself is God honouring. Even with such employment, it is possible to live a life displaying the fruit of the spirit.

I think it goes without saying that there are some occupations which a Christian would be wise to avoid. If my work contributes to the well being of mankind or provides a helpful service to my neighbour, so well and good. But if my work will bring hurt or cause problems in health, or in some other way, have a detrimental affect upon my fellow men, then this cannot really be acceptable and our own spiritual well being will be affected adversely.

However, a good job well done is acceptable to the Lord and, if offered to Him daily will also bring some satisfaction to us. There usually is the opportunity to make a direct witness too to our work mates. No matter how menial or dirty the work may be it can be honouring to God.

Yet there are those who feel compelled or 'called' to take upon themselves definite, extra special work, and whilst this may provide 'a living'., which of course it necessary, see their work being more than just a job to earn a living.

It is rather a vocation, and they *were born* to follow this way. Immediately there springs to mind those engaged in the medical or teaching profession. There are others of course who feel strongly that in a way they had no choice but to follow their career and fulfil such a role in life. They also would feel their life would be unfulfilled if they didn't follow this 'call.'

Seeking to fulfil God's plan for the Christian will include asking for direction concerning one's employment and if this is a real vocation, even if it is not particularly remunerative, this should be accepted when God reveals it to us.

I would not dare to suggest one calling is any greater or more important than another but near the top of the list if not *the* top, surely none could be more demanding or rewarding than that of a Minister of Religion. Today most churches regrettably are suffering, in common with each other by having insufficient candidates for the Ministry. I do not believe it is because God is not calling, but for some reason people are not responding to the Call. Whatever the reason might be it surely is the responsibility of every Christian – should God call – to give this serious consideration.

Can there be a more deserving case than sharing, in a very positive way the saving work of the Saviour? Since the church was born, indeed, long before this took place and in the worship of God by the Jews, people have been ordained or commissioned into full time leadership of the Faith. They have had, handed down, one from another the oracles of the Faith, albeit beset with failures from time to time, but nevertheless this has been part of their work as well as leading others into a knowledge of God.

It is an awesome responsibility of course, but what an honour to be chosen by God to be His helper!

How does a person know God is calling *them?* This may come in a variety of ways.

There are those who, with no preparation at all and even with no church loyalties have suddenly become aware that they must give up all plans to become business people and give their lives to the church. Their *Call* could so easily have come to them before their *conversion.* This is one of the surprises of God. He doesn't stick to what we might call normal or orthodox ways!

Many of course have through the cultivation of spiritual sensitivity, over a period of time established a relationship with God (which we have continually made reference to) and have responded to a prompting from Him.

Others may have become aware of a need and felt they could help meet this need. Still others feel the responsibility for ensuring the continued safe journey through time of the Gospel and have wanted to do their part.

Whichever way He might choose, if God wants anyone to serve Him in this way, He will use one method or another to make this clear to that person and it is up to them then to respond. He never forces His will upon anyone.

It has to be said there are many people who in the days of their youth heard the Call yet decided to go their own way or for some other reason have not responded as they feel they ought. They may have become terrific leaders in their local church, have a very nice home and family, successful business yet, despite all this, there is a very real regret deep in the heart because they didn't respond as they ought to God's voice. I have seen people weep because of this. These good folk need to share this with the Lord. It may be too late now to redress the situation, but if ones life is still spent in glorifying His name we can be assured He accepts this and bears no grudge. Don't live your life under a cloud of guilt, let Him deal with it.

The particular gifts or qualifications or the lack of them is never a barrier to God's call, although if we are competent in anyway it is amazing how they can be used in His service. Jesus called ordinary men and women to become His first disciples with some of them being fishermen. He told them that in future they would 'catch men.' (Matt. 4: 18-22)

It may be of course that He does not require this from us after all, but we must still be ready to assume responsibility for local leadership should this be needed. It does appear there is a reluctance to assume responsibility in any way these days – not just in the church either. Many youth organisations are suffering in this way. People want to be free, have no ties, do their own thing. Despite the ever increasing amount of leisure time people have these days there is not a great haste to use just a little of this to help others or get involved.

The Christian really has to avoid such an attitude. To say the least it is unfair to expect others to carry a too heavy a load and at the other end of the scale, a lack of leaders endangers the witness of the Church.

There is untold blessing and happiness when giving, which, although not particularly sought after does come to those who are prepared to give their time to benefit others. *'It is more blessed to give than to receive.'* (Acts 20: 35) This is true when giving in other ways too.

For so many Christians, the idea of God, first of all to give His life in order to reconcile us unto Himself is far too wonderful for words. Then, to become part of His family and enter a loving, helpful fellowship is an added bonus. But then, to crown it all, to be counted worthy to be called to help shoulder the great responsibility of representing Him as leaders in the church is an indescribable privilege.

From time to time I have heard Christians speak of their discipleship as a *sacrifice.* They point out various things they have done or have had to deny themselves of in order to fulfil the will of God in their lives. Maybe referring to giving up a very lucrative career, or a big house, promotion or something.

I feel there is something sad about such an attitude because when we compare (if we dare) the sacrifice *He* made, how can we, in any way consider the little bit we have given up with that. In any case, have we not proved that what little we do give up He repays or compensates more than a hundred times more?

No, there should be no reluctance to give talents, money or time to God. The Bible says the *'Lord loves a cheerful giver'* (2 Cor. 9:7)

Of course, millions of people do live their lives with no reference to God and certainly have no thought whatever of fulfilling God's will, and are quite happy. But I would venture to say that they are unaware that they have in fact been robbed of that deep down joy and sense of real purpose which is such a tragedy. Those of us therefore who are chosen and *'Walking in the light'* (1 John 1: 7) should hold on to this at all costs. Our enthusiasm could well be the means of bringing another into this same experience.

'Doing the will of God, doing the will of God.
The best thing I know
In this world below,
Is doing the will of God'

9. Goal!

Michael Parkinson, the well known and well loved T.V. presenter recalled, as we entered the new millennium some of the highlights of his programme over the years. One of these included an interview with the 100 year old Commissioner Catherine Booth, a granddaughter of the founder of The Salvation Army, William Booth.

As it turned out (and we half expected this,) it was Commissioner Catherine who did the interviewing in front of an estimated T.V. audience of 18,000,000 people. Michael appeared to be in awe of the centenarian, particularly so when she challenged him about his own standing with God! I have an idea he hasn't got over this yet!

However the question was asked, " Commissioner, are you looking forward to going to Heaven?" She replied, "I am – but I don't want to go just yet. I want to live my life to the full before then."

I link this interview with a personal testimony I heard when, as a young Lieutenant I listened to a Salvation Army Brigadier who had served in Cuba in charge of a large children's home. She stated during one public meeting that, " I am so glad I invited Christ into my life when I was just a young girl, and He has given me such a rewarding and full life. Even if there was no such place as Heaven, following Jesus in *this life* is still the best thing anyone can do."

I agree with both these ladies who, by the way I believe are now with their Lord and enjoying the fullness of His presence. Serving, living, enjoying life with Christ is the best thing anyone can possibly do despite the ups and downs which everyone experiences. Life has so much to offer when shared with Him and so of course there is no desperate hurry to leave it. Every day brings its own challenges, its own joys and making the best of this on every occasion brings a fulfilling life.

Yes Brigadier, I agree with you. It is worth being a Christian here and now even if there was no such place as Heaven.

But there is! *Hallelujah!* The pages in this book have all been concerned with living life as it is now, facing problems and dealing with them. Reference has been made from time to time about the 'here-after' but we have not discussed at any length what this really means.

This final chapter then concentrates upon the next world – which is all part – the biggest part – of the treasure God has, through Christ prepared for us.

If Good Friday dealt with our sin and its consequences, Easter Sunday confirms there is eternal life for those who believe.

What evidence do we have that such a state exists? Will there be room for everyone? Where is Heaven? How will it happen? and so on.

First of all, *is* there life after death? Is there any evidence around for us to consider which supports such a claim?

It has to be said straight away that if anyone is searching for some tangible, physical evidence such a state does exist then they may as well give up here and now. Apart from Jesus, no one has ever been and then returned to earth with a definite 'yes' about such a place.

However there are other senses which come into play and these are most convincing.

For just a moment, let us put to one side Biblical references and seek some confirmation from other sources.

Number one surely is our own instinct. We must not be in too big a hurry to dismiss this just as wishful thinking. Of course it is a nice thought but can we lay any store by it? Obviously, when there has been bereavement in a family and someone particularly loved and cherished has died, there is this longing, this wish that one day, they will be with them again and the separation is healed. Speaking as I have with so many, many people at such a sad time – and not all of them professing Christians – a very large percentage feel *instinctively* death is not the end even though they have no idea as to what the next life might be like.

Common sense suggests to many what a waste it would be for all the knowledge and wisdom and expertise which has been gained in a person's life over the years to suddenly come to an abrupt halt through death. What would be the point?

Of recent years I have, in common with others watched on T.V. or read with real interest of men and women who claim to have died, some even being issued with death certificates, yet speak of an 'out of body' experience. They speak of dying and then find themselves looking down upon 'their body'. They tell of travelling down a tunnel toward a brilliant light at the end. They speak about the feeling of peace and tranquillity. They tell of the beautiful 'land' they were able to glimpse before returning to indwell their body again and come 'back to life'. They further speak of death now holding no fear for them for 'it is only like going through a door into something wonderful.'

Ancient religions have some sort of afterlife as part of their beliefs. These may not compare as favourable as the Christian belief but they point to the fact that instinctively mankind 'feels in his bones' death is not the end. These religions by the way existed a long time before Christianity.

We however are thinking along the Christian way and so naturally look to the words Jesus uttered about this 'place.'

To record at this juncture every reference Jesus made to Heaven and the afterlife would be an exercise in itself. We will however take a few, but the diligent reader should carefully read the Gospels to have a wider picture.

The well known verse *'For God so loved the world, that He gave His only son, that whosoever believes in Him should not perish but have ever lasting life'* (John 3: 16) cannot be misunderstood. Its message is quite clear and plain. The promise that Jesus is going to prepare a place for the believer is also quite clear needing very little if any clarification. (John 14: 2-3)

When Jesus was confronted by a group of the Jewish leaders about life after death, He drew their attention to Moses's experience with the 'burning bush' (Exodus 3: 6) when God refers to being the God of Abraham, Isaac and Jacob all of whom had died centuries before. Jesus stated, *'God is not the God of the dead, but of the living, for to Him all are alive.'* (Luke 20: 37-38)

Paul, heads his list of useless adversaries which might try to separate us from God with the word *death,* and then goes on to say that nothing can cause such separation – we are safe and secure with Him. (Romans 8: 38-39)

The Biblical references quoted and added to a multitude more all find a resting place in the heart of the believer, confirming over an over again that there is most certainly a life after this one.

Will there be room enough for everyone? Is Heaven big enough to 'house' the untold millions who lived long before our day, let alone those who are alive today?

Of course it is difficult, indeed impossible to picture a place which can accommodate so many although we may be surprised to find there will not be as many there as we might at first think, a point we will enlarge upon a little later in this chapter. We naturally think about life as we see it in this world with its limitations and boundaries. The measuring rule we are trying to bring into play may be workable in this world of *time* but it will be quite different when *eternity* becomes a reality, we can be sure of this.

Having made such a statement though we only have to ask ourselves the unanswerable question 'how big is space?' and we will soon see that the necessary room to accommodate is of little importance or warrants serious consideration.

This brings us to another thought. Where is Heaven, and what will it be like?

In a very real sense, and Jesus spoke about this, Heaven first of all is within us. (Luke 17: 21) This surely is what prompts every man's instinct and gives the inner feeling Heaven exists. It becomes more real and more insistent when a person has come into a knowledge of Christ as Saviour. The *real* Christian therefore has already caught a glimpse of his final destiny, albeit in a most limited way, yet such a glimpse excites the spirit and there is real, eager anticipation to see it in all its glory.

All references suggest most strongly that Heaven will be the most beautiful, wonderful, happy, challenging sin-free place imaginable. In fact, it is far beyond our imagination and like all spiritual subjects, no language on this earth can come anywhere near to adequately describe it.

The writers in the Bible, when trying to give some description as to what Heaven is like refer to the most precious metals such as gold and silver, and precious stones too which are costly to mankind and this world but commonplace in Heaven. One such reference speaks of streets being paved with gold. (Revelation 21: 21)

We are told, and this surely is such wonderful news, 'He will wipe away every tear from their eyes. There will be no more death, or mourning, or crying or pain, for the old order of things has passed away.' (Revelation 21: 4)

Now where Heaven is situated in the universe is another unanswerable question and a mystery. There are those who feel strongly it is in fact some far distant planet! We need to keep in mind that passing through the door of death, the world we enter is a *spiritual* world and does not conform to the natural laws of time and material which we have known all our lives and recognise with our senses. It could well be that when our eyes are *really* opened, and we can see clearly, Heaven may be around us *now*.

Of all the sights to behold the most wonderful surely, which will outshine all else in Heaven is the face of our loving Father for we will be in the fullness of His presence.

It will be the complete fulfilment of the relationship began on earth but will eclipse all that has happened in life by the glory of His full presence. There will be no need to have faith or hope for anything, for faith and hope will have found their destiny. But as Paul writes in his famous chapter in the first book of Corinthians, the greatest thing which will last is *Love.* (1 Cor. 13: 13)

So, who will go to this wonderful place? Can every human being rest in the knowledge that in the end, *all* mankind will have a place reserved for them?

Most certainly this was God's intension. He is, after all the Creator and Father of all men and does not will that anyone should perish (2 Peter 3: 9) Yet, with the entrance of sin into the world at the very beginning, such an automatic right was forfeited. We turn back to chapter one in this book to discover reference has already been made to the great gulf between God and man, goodness and evil and this brought with it ultimate death – with pain and suffering en-route.

Because there is absolutely no place for sin in Heaven, and in the presence of the righteous God, (Rev. 21: 8) our sin has to be dealt with. The favoured place once enjoyed by God and man has to be re-established. There needs to be reconciliation between the Father and His child, and all this *before* leaving *this* world. God has prepared a place only for prepared people!

When the Bible speaks about being 'saved' it means escaping the consequences of our sin – and this includes being denied entry into Heaven.

The only way this can be done is through Jesus. The whole purpose of His coming was to do just this for us. There is no other name under Heaven whereby we can be saved (Acts 4: 12) If there had been any other way, it would not have been necessary for Jesus to give Himself on that fateful day to be mercilessly murdered on the cross.

The purpose for the existence of the Church is to tell out this message. The Gospel story is one both of good news and warning. All creation is bound for the place the Devil has prepared for those who choose to reject God's plan. God has done all He can to stop this but will not *force* His will upon anyone. Having respect for man's free-will, he is left to decide for himself as to where his final destiny will be. According to the Bible, it is much harder to choose God's way than the Devil's hence there will be comparatively few who will, in the end find their place in Heaven. (Matt. 7: 13 & 14)

The reader should take note that it is not *God* who sends a man to hell. It is man who decides *himself* to reject God's plan to save him. This doesn't contradict the statement that God is a God of love, on the contrary, the escape route has come from this very loving God in order to avoid eternal unhappiness.

Our goal is Heaven. God has done all He can to ensure we will reach that place, but this will not happen unless we do our part.

Part and parcel of the afterlife, and spoken about and referred to so often in the New Testament is the return of Jesus to earth at the end of the world.

Scientists are constantly telling us that one day this planet Earth will come to an end. The most recent T.V. programmes suggest strongly that it will be sucked into what is commonly known as a 'black hole' and so will be obliterated.

I am no scientist and like so many 'ordinary' people, wonder how they come to such a conclusion. However, The Bible clearly states that in the last days, there will be the destruction of all that we see, the likes of which has never been seen before. The whole of chapter 24 of Matthew speaks about this, as does the book of Daniel and Revelation. It is not an easy subject to understand and great scholars have disagreed upon certain points but one thing *is* agreed – there will be an end to this world.

It is the time when Jesus will come again, not as a helpless baby as He did in Bethlehem but as the triumphant and risen Lord. (Acts 1: 10 & 11) Every eye will see Him, even those who caused His death (Rev. 1: 7) This will be the time when all will be judged and if their names are not written in the 'Book of Life' then they are to be cast out from the presence of God and all goodness, to an existence which is devoid of anything good and lovely and beautiful. It will be hell indeed.

Jesus, when walking the earth as man spoke about the separation of the sheep from the goats, (Matt. 25: 33) In this same chapter of Matthew He further speaks about the separation of the good and the bad. (Matt. 25: 34-36) The same theme is spoken about with the good seed and the weeds. (Matt. 13: 24-29 and 36-40)

There are many other references to such a separation all indicating this is something which needs to be taken seriously.

On the Judgement Day, mankind will find himself on one side or the other. There will be no neutral stand.

Of course people put this to one side, or to the back of their minds, but we ignore this at our peril. Preparation needs to be made now, whilst there is time and not wait until it is too late.

The ***only*** way we can be certain to enter Heaven is by

believing in the Lord Jesus Christ. (Acts 16:31)

When will all this happen is a question asked over and over again, despite the fact Jesus stated quite clearly that no one knows. (Matt. 24: 42; 44 & 25: 13; Mark 13: 31-37, Acts 1:7) There are individuals and 'fringe' Christian organisations who have tried to set a date. There are some sects which have actually published a number of dates, one to supersede the others when they have been proved to be wrong. I have no intention of foolishly following their example. As far as the Church is concerned – and I am part of this – the words of Jesus are sufficient. What we need to do is be ready for this momentous happening, making sure we are on the Lord's side.

If we don't, it really will be too late, there is no second chance. The Devil will have satisfactorily completed the task he set out to accomplish. He will have thwarted God's plan. He will have dashed to pieces the hope of reconciliation. He will have ensured there will be a great company of people joining him in that last place of indescribable horror, from which there is no escape. He will have committed *'Daylight Robbery'*

'Most aweful truth, and is it so, must all the world the harvest know?
Must all before the Judge appear?
Then for the harvest, O prepare!
To love my sins, a saint appear, to grow with wheat and be tare,
May serve me while on earth below, where tares and wheat together grow……'.

We now come to those questions which, at first appear to be unanswerable. With a little searching of the Scriptures however we can become aware to some extent what our hearts and minds are seeking.

When we die – and all mankind must die apart from those who will be alive when Christ returns to earth – where does our spirit go? Different religions may offer different ideas but looking into the Bible, and as Christians this is where we obtain our information, it suggests there is a place *before* the final

Heaven.

On that first Good Friday, there were three men who died by being crucified on Calvary. On either side of Jesus were two criminals. One of these riled upon Jesus and demanded that He sets Himself free from the cross and take these other two with Him. Before Jesus can answer, the other thief rebuked his companion, and called upon Jesus to remember him when Jesus came to His kingdom. (Luke 23: 39-42)

It is interesting to speculate as to whether these two men had ever met Jesus before and even heard His preaching or perhaps witnessed His miracles. Obviously they knew of Him although it is interesting that they held opposing interpretations about His claims. The one held the view that His powers were to be used to exert His authority for His own benefit and use force to this end too. The second man however had some idea of the deeper mission of Jesus and its spiritual implications hence his dying plea. It is the answer Jesus gave to this man, however which we are considering. "Today, you will be with me in Paradise." (Luke 23: 43) Note, Jesus did not say you will be with me in *Heaven* but in *Paradise.* Just three days later, on the first Easter Sunday morning, Mary came to the tomb in order to embalm His body but we read He was not there. In desperation, Mary turns to go back home, deeply distressed, but as she turns she sees a man she thought was the gardener. Responding to his question about why she was so upset, the gardener simply said, "Mary" and Mary recognised Him to be Jesus. Jesus then told her not to touch Him because He hadn't yet returned to Heaven. (John 20: 10-17) Now, if Jesus, by His own words admitted He had not yet gone to Heaven, where did He go when He died and where had He been for last couple of days? According to what was said to the thief, He had been to Paradise, and the repentant man had gone with Him.

When we die we move into this next stage of our existence to await the final Judgement Day at the end of time.

Of course we are in the presence of our Lord as indicated to the thief and to His disciples (Matthew 28: 20) This is a real comfort to we believers and takes away any fear death might hold.

The Bible speaks about those who have died in Jesus as being asleep to await the time Jesus will 'awaken' us to join Him in the skies. We cannot be sure what, if any consciousness we might possess before Jesus comes again. There are those who believe we will be actively engaged in preaching to those who have died and who never knew Jesus, giving them the same choice we had on earth in either accepting or rejecting Jesus. Others believe we become spirits of influence in this world, helping the Lord's mission by supporting His children here and now. I am afraid it is not clearly defined and maybe is left to speculation – if that is what we choose to do. As far as I am concerned, I am not unduly worried what, if anything I will be *doing,* as long as I am in the presence of my Lord. This is all that really matters to me. I am also content in the knowledge that I am at last going to spend eternity with Him in Heaven.

Do we lose our identity? I think not. We are told we will be changed – different to what we are now (1 Corinthians 15: 20-22; 51-58) yet still recognisable as was Jesus. (John 20 & John 21) Moses and Elijah too even though they had died many, many years before were known (Mark 9: 5) The immortal body might be quite different to the one we have now but the essential personality and characteristics we retain will make sure others will know who we are as we will know them. It would be a funny place if this were not so.

It has been said that life really is one of relationships, and if we think about this for a moment or two I am sure we could do nothing else but agree. Without any kind of relationship, not only would it be a lonely existence but for almost every living person intolerable – hardly a life.

I heard some years ago an Anglican Bishop state that of all terms to describe the death of a human being, The Salvation Army uses the most hopeful and optimistic one. *'Promoted to Glory'.* In other words, it only gets better.

The relationship with our Lord, which begins on this earth is what all of this is about. A relationship which grows in its beauty and loveliness each day. A relationship which becomes more and more precious and one which is not severed by death – on the contrary – it will really come into its own when we open the door to take us from this life in to the next.

'When Christ shall come with shouts of acclamation,
To take me home, what joy will fill my heart!
Then I will bow in humble adoration,
And there proclaim, my God, how great Thou art!

Are you sure you will be part of this? Or maybe, despite all that has been said, you are going to allow that thief – the devil to steal this priceless gift from under your nose. That really would be *Daylight Robbery!*

Epilogue

Sharing thoughts about certain problems I have had to sort out in my own mind in order to ensure my experience of God remains a real and satisfying experience has proved to be an interesting, even exciting exercise. It has caused me to look again at the foundations of my faith. The conclusion being I have every confidence in the living God and His plan for me.

I need to emphasise however such thoughts and conclusions are *mine,* and it is quite likely they will not provide satisfactory answers for everyone.

It must be said too that revelation from God is an on-going experience and it is more than possible that future days will cause me to adjust drastically or even change completely certain statements as recorded in *'Daylight Robbery'.* I am not worried about this but rather welcome further light as it comes and from what ever source, being ever open to the revelation which comes to the sincere seeker after the truth.

In *'Daylight Robbery',* Scripture references have been purposely kept to a minimum. Having used many books which have been 'swamped' by too many such references I have found on a number occasions my interest being drained away. Listening to others I discover I am not alone. I wanted to avoid this at all costs yet at the same time get my point home.

However, if these writings have caused others to find more interest in The Bible and even more than this, have encouraged a healthier experience of God, I am pleased.

God has made such wonderful provision for His children but He can't *make* us eat. We do this ourselves. It is a real partnership. We are workers together with God. (2 Cor. 6: 1) When we do co-operate in this way how blessed we are. Having 'scratched' the proverbial surface of ways to a more fulfilling religious experience, I would urge you to go deeper. Discover the treasure trove awaiting you and under no circumstances whatever, allow Satan to snatch it away. You can do it. God has promised that there is *no temptation* too difficult for us to overcome. (1 Cor. 10: 13)

I pray you will know something of the security and peace which comes to all who truly believe. I trust too you will be content to leave yourself in the loving arms of your Heavenly Father, knowing that any unanswered question will pose no threat to such contentment.

'May the Lord bless and protect you;
May the Lord's face radiate with joy because of you;
May He be gracious to you, show you His favour,
And give you His peace.'

(Numbers 6: 24-26)

****